TOMB RAIDERS

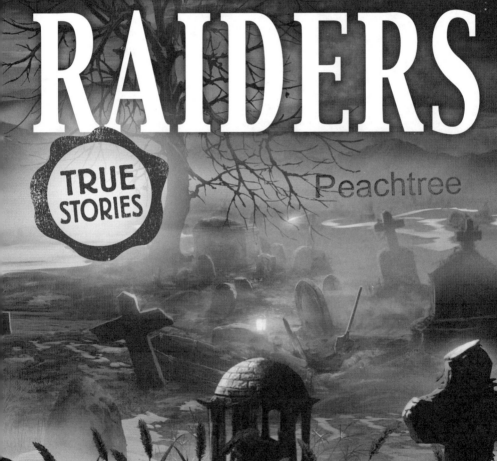

TRUE STORIES

Peachtree

Real Tales of Grave Robberies

JUDY DODGE CUMMINGS

Nomad Press
A division of Nomad Communications
10 9 8 7 6 5 4 3 2 1

This book was manufactured by CGB Printers,
North Mankato, Minnesota, United States
February 2018, Job #240586
ISBN Softcover: 978-1-61930-622-6
ISBN Hardcover: 978-1-61930-620-2

Educational Consultant, Marla Conn

Questions regarding the ordering of this book should be addressed to
Nomad Press
2456 Christian St.
White River Junction, VT 05001
www.nomadpress.net

Printed in the United States.

Contents

Titles in the **Mystery & Mayhem** Series

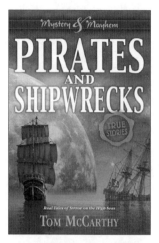

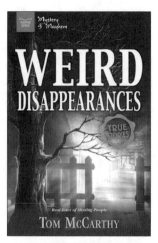

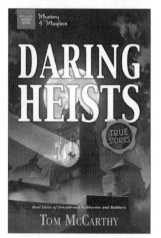

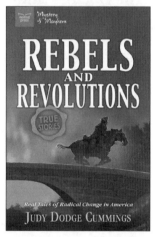

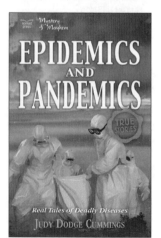

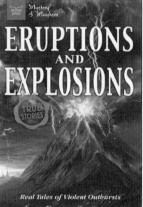

Check out more titles at www.nomadpress.net

Introduction

Silence Disturbed

When the dead are laid to rest, prayers are chanted and hymns sung. The coffin is lowered into the ground and the burial vault is sealed. Mourners dry their tears and return to their lives. Silence falls over the graveyard. Bodies are left to slumber for eternity in their final resting places.

But the dead do not always rest easy.

Sometimes, their peace is shattered when grave robbers come to pay their respects. On a moonless night, these shadowy figures creep into the graveyard. In some cases, only a day or two has passed since the dead person was buried, but in others, more than a millennium has gone by.

The thieves exchange hurried whispers. A match is struck, a lantern lit. When the burglars find the grave they seek, they plunge a shovel into the ground or slice a saw through a padlocked vault. Perhaps a sarcophagus is revealed. A crowbar slips between the cover and the casket, and with a painful creak, the lid rises.

Tomb Raiders

The air of centuries rushes out as light races in. The grave robbers look down upon the face of someone no longer of this world.

Tomb raiders risk the anger of the law, the dead person's loved ones, and the spirit world. What do they seek that is worth such dangers?

British colonists in Jamestown, Virginia, were ravenous when they dug up the dead during the "Starving Time" in the winter of 1609–1610. A severe drought, hostile neighbors, and poor management by colony leaders caused a food shortage. The colonists consumed everything they could find, from rats to toadstools.

Desperate to survive, some settlers turned to the graves of those already gone, which lay just outside the fort's walls.

Medical students in New York City had plenty of food in 1788, but not enough bodies. To become a doctor, the students had to learn human anatomy, and the best way to do this was by dissecting corpses. Called "resurrectionists," the students dug up the dead from the African Burial Ground and the potter's field outside the city limits. The fresher the corpse, the better. Authorities turned a blind eye to this body snatching until a student went too far and stole a white woman's corpse from a church graveyard.

That's when the city exploded in riots.

Even the tombs of the famous are not safe. In 1876, a gang formed a plot to steal the corpse of President Lincoln and hold it for ransom. Tipped off by an informant, the Secret Service interrupted the thieves just as they were prying open the president's coffin. After this near miss, Lincoln's corpse was moved from hiding place to hiding place for the next 20 years to protect it from grave robbers.

Sometimes, grave robbers themselves do the work of archaeologists and uncover ancient treasures. In 1881, a goat belonging to a thief stumbled into a shaft in a cliff in the Valley of the Kings in Egypt. When the man lowered himself into the shaft to save his goat, he discovered a cache of more than 50 royal mummies, including some of the most famous pharaohs of ancient Egypt.

Tomb raiders often seek the treasure buried beside the body rather than the corpse itself. That was the case when riches were discovered in a pyramid built by the Moche culture outside the village of Sipán, Peru. In 1987, the unearthing of treasure sparked a gold rush that pit poor peasants against archaeologists.

Read on to learn more about these true tales of tomb raiders. Be prepared to encounter adventure, intrigue, suspense, and some ghostly, ghastly history.

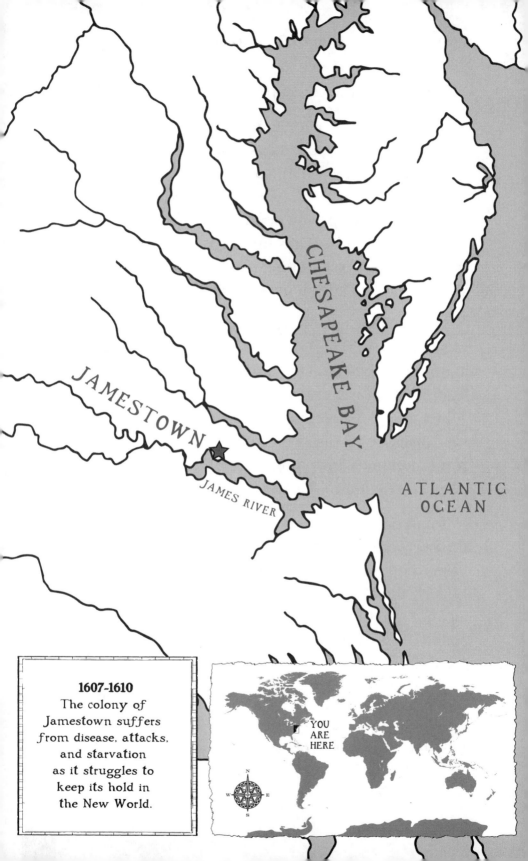

CHESAPEAKE BAY

JAMESTOWN

JAMES RIVER

ATLANTIC OCEAN

1607-1610

The colony of Jamestown suffers from disease, attacks, and starvation as it struggles to keep its hold in the New World.

YOU ARE HERE

N
W E
S

1585	1606	1620
Roanoke Island colony is established and fails in what is now North Carolina	The English first settle Jamestown	The Pilgrims land in what becomes Plymouth Colony

Chapter One

When Bones Speak

As the sun slipped below the horizon on June 1, 1609, a fleet of ships rode the tide away from England. About 500 passengers watched their homeland disappear, among them a 14-year-old girl whose name has been lost to history.

The ships plowed through the vast Atlantic Ocean, their destination the fledging British colony in Jamestown, Virginia. Whatever hopes and dreams the young girl carried as she sailed toward a new life soon became nightmares.

For 400 years, her story was swallowed by the past, just like her name.

Then, in 2012, archaeologists unearthed the girl's final resting place. They named her Jane Doe. Etched in Jane's bones is the story of a gruesome grave robbery. This theft was not for greed or power, but for life itself.

Jamestown colony was doomed from the start. The king of Great Britain, James I, granted a charter to a group of investors, who formed the Virginia Company to build a settlement in North America. The company had three goals: to establish a permanent colony, locate a water route between the Atlantic and Pacific Oceans, and find gold.

On December 20, 1606, three ships set sail from England carrying 104 men and boys. The vessels carried enough provisions to cover a two-month ocean crossing and six months in America. Time enough, the Virginia Company believed, for settlers to plant and harvest crops and develop trade relations with the local people.

These calculations were wildly off the mark, and the Jamestown settlers would pay dearly for this mistake.

Five months later, on April 26, 1607, a sailor cried, "Land ho," as the ship entered the Chesapeake Bay. A landing party of 30 men led by Captain Christopher Newport waded ashore that balmy morning.

Settler George Percy wrote that he was "almost ravished" by the sight of "faire meadows and goodly tall trees." The men explored all day, confident they had found paradise in this land they called Virginia.

All too soon, paradise would be hell on earth.

———◆———

The area of Virginia that the colonists entered already had a name and a leader. Tsenacomoco, also called the Powhatan Confederacy, was an alliance of 30 Native American tribes led by a supreme chief—Wahunsunacock. The English would come to know him as Chief Powhatan. Roughly 14,000 Powhatan people lived in small towns dotting the high ground along the rivers that fed into the area around the Chesapeake Bay.

Each town was home to a few hundred people who lived in barrel-shaped houses fashioned from bent saplings. Women tended fields of corn and beans. The men hunted wild game in forests of chestnut and elm trees.

The Chesapeake region was a land of beauty and usually full of food. But the year before the English arrived had been different. The rains refused to fall. Corn and bean crops shriveled in the fields. Hunters returned home empty-handed. The Powhatan were not eager to welcome newcomers with so little food.

At dusk that first day, when Captain Newport's landing party returned to the beach, the native people attacked. One settler wrote later, "There came the savages creeping upon all fours from the hills like bears, with their bows in their mouths." The English scurried back to their ships. This first encounter between the settlers and Native Americans did not bode well for the colony's future.

The settlers were counting on trade with the Native Americans to supplement their food supplies. The English could not have known this, but they had landed in Virginia at the beginning of the worst drought the region had seen in nearly 800 years.

As the drought dragged on and the Powhatan ran short of food, they had nothing to trade.

———◆———

After the attack, the British fleet sailed northwest on a broad river the settlers called the James River.

The seven members of Jamestown's council kept their eyes peeled for the perfect spot to build the colony.

The land needed natural defenses to protect against invaders. It had to be located near water deep enough for ships to anchor close to shore.

Also, the Virginia Company had insisted the land be unoccupied. Investors had no interest in starting a conflict with the native people.

On May 12, 1607, the council found what it was looking for. A peninsula jutted into the James River about 30 miles from the Chesapeake Bay. Only a narrow strip of land connected it to the mainland.

This isthmus was surrounded by an impassable swamp, and the shoreline was shielded by thick woods. These were perfect natural defenses. The river was so deep below the peninsula's bank that ships could tie up to trees on the shoreline. Best of all, there were no signs of people. The British named their settlement Jamestown after their king, and they moved in.

There were good reasons no one lived on the peninsula, but by the time the settlers figured out what these reasons were, it was too late.

Laborers cleared trees. Soldiers scouted the mainland. Farmers tilled the soil and planted seeds.

However, the Atlantic crossing had taken three months longer than the Virginia Company had planned. In what was left of the growing season, the colonists would not be able to harvest enough food to last through winter.

The time had come to negotiate a trade deal with the locals.

On May 21, 1607, Captain Newport led a small group of men on an expedition to meet the neighbors. They also hoped to discover the riches of the New World. The group encountered several villages of friendly native people, but there were no signs of either gold or a water route to the Pacific Ocean.

When the expedition returned to Jamestown, the men found chaos. Two hundred Powhatan warriors had attacked the settlement, killing a teenage boy and wounding 17 men. The president of Jamestown's council had narrowly escaped death when an arrow passed through his beard. Captain Newport ordered a fort built immediately.

During the next 19 days, the settlers dodged arrows from Native Americans, who hid behind trees and inside swaths of tall grasses. Working double-time, the settlers managed to erect a triangle-shaped

palisade from tree trunks and mount cannons
on each corner. Inside the palisade, they built a
storehouse, a small church, and a handful of cabins.

The time then came for Captain Newport to sail
back to England with two of the ships. He promised
to return in early 1608 with more supplies. The
council drafted a report for Captain Newport to
deliver to King James and the Virginia Company.

The leaders tried to put a good face on their
situation. "We are fortified well against the Indians,"
they wrote. "We have sown a good store of wheat . . .
we have built some houses. . . . With God's help, the
colony would just get . . . better and better."

But the report ended on a note of desperation. The
councilmen begged the Virginia Company to send
much-needed supplies quickly. "Otherwise, to our
greatest and last griefs," the colony might fail.

On June 22, 1607, Captain Newport and the crew
sailed around the bend in the river and disappeared
from view. Anxiety must have flooded the hearts of
the colonists as they watched their link to England
vanish.

Then, a message arrived from Chief Powhatan,
telling the British he had ordered all attacks on
the fort to stop. The end of the harassment was a
relief, but peace would not fill anyone's belly. Chief
Powhatan's message had said nothing about trade.
The settlers needed a lot of corn each week to

meet their needs. Their own crops were not ready to harvest, and the Native Americans could not be counted on to supply the settlers.

By August, the colonists were getting only 500 calories a day. It was a starvation diet.

The settlers began to die, but it was not hunger that killed them—at least, not at first. The colonists finally discovered why no one lived on the Jamestown peninsula. The location was deadly. The swamp surrounding the isthmus was home to malaria-carrying mosquitos. Malaria is a disease that saps a person's strength.

Another problem with the location was that there were no freshwater springs on the peninsula. The settlers had been drinking from the James River since they arrived.

The water was poisonous.

The river was deep and fast in spring when the colony was established, but by the middle of summer, the water level had dropped 15 feet. Salty Atlantic tides flowed upstream and sediment and organic waste became trapped around the peninsula.

Colonist George Percy described the James River as "full of slime and filth." The diseases of dysentery and typhoid from water crawling with bacteria killed dozens of people.

Captain Newport kept his word and returned with supplies and another 120 settlers in January 1608. When he landed, only 38 of the original 104 colonists were still alive. Then, another tragedy struck. Newport's crew had barely finished unloading their ships when a fire swept through the fort, destroying most of the provisions they had sailed 6,000 miles to bring.

Now, Jamestown's real nightmare began.

Captain Newport not only brought more colonists from England, he also arrived with high expectations from Virginia Company. The Jamestown project was costing Virginia Company investors a lot of money, and so far they had not seen a profit. Where was the trade route to the Pacific? Where were the mines full of gold and silver?

Company executives threatened Captain Newport. If he did not return to London with something valuable, the company would cut off supplies to the colonists.

Virginia had no gold and silver, but it did have forests. Captain Newport ordered the colonists to chop down trees. Settlers who should have been tilling fields or hunting game for themselves were instead busy sawing boards for Virginia Company.

On April 10, 1608, Captain Newport departed for London with a cargo of lumber. He returned in September with yet more colonists and another demand from the Virginia Company.

Look harder for gold.

Also, in September 1608, Captain John Smith took over as council president. Although arrogant, Smith was also practical and skilled. He negotiated aggressively with Chief Powhatan for food and established strict discipline inside the fort.

Under Captain Smith's rule that "He that shall not work, shall not eat," Jamestown finally made progress toward self-sufficiency.

The colonists built 20 more houses, repaired the church, and raised 60 pigs and more than 500 chickens. To please the Virginia Company, they produced barrels of pitch, tar, and soap, which Captain Newport transported to England in January 1609. It was not gold, but at least these were goods the company could sell.

To improve health, Captain Smith ordered a well dug inside the fort. The settlers finally had what they thought was "sweet water."

1609 map of Virginia as described by Captain John Smith
photo credit: Library of Congress

In truth, the water was far from sweet.

The fort's latrines were located too close to the new well. The drinking water became contaminated with toxic bacteria.

Mother Nature also dealt Jamestown a brutal blow as the Northern Hemisphere plunged into one of the coldest spells in centuries. Colonists who had come to Virginia expecting a tropical climate now shivered through frost and flurries.

To make the situation even more miserable, when John Smith checked the fort's corn supply, he found it "half rotten, the rest so consumed [by] the many thousand rats that we knew not how to keep the little we had. . . . This did drive us all to our wits end." Hunger settled in for a long visit.

This was the environment young Jane Doe was heading into when she sailed from England on the colony's third resupply mission in the summer of 1609. This fleet had nine ships—eight small vessels to transport colonists and the large flagship, *Sea Venture*, which carried enough provisions to keep Jamestown fed for a full year.

But fate was not finished with Jamestown.

On July 25, the fleet sailed into a hurricane. The storm battered the ships, hurling people into the sea, lashing sails, and splitting masts. One passenger described the storm as, "A hell of darkness turned black upon us. . . ." When the skies finally cleared, the *Sea Venture* and all its provisions had vanished.

During the next few weeks, six of the nine ships limped to Virginia. The survivors of the storm—hundreds of men, women, and children—stumbled to shore. Some were injured, others were diseased, and all were hungry.

Crushing disappointment must have fallen on the settlers as they watched these new arrivals enter the fort. Instead of delivering salvation, the seas had tossed ashore more mouths to feed.

One of those mouths belonged to Jane Doe.

A strong, capable leader was needed to steer the colony through this crisis. But Jamestown had no such person. John Smith had left Virginia. His blunt, bullying style had upset his fellow councilmen. George Percy described Smith as a "an ambitious, unworthy and vainglorious fellow."

In October 1609, John Smith's gunpowder bag ignited while he was asleep on a boat. The explosion tore a 10-inch square of flesh from his torso and thighs.

Some historians suspect John Smith was the target of an attempted assassination by other council members. The explosion did not kill the opinionated leader, but he returned to England for treatment and never set foot in Virginia again.

George Percy replaced John Smith as colony president, but he was not up to the task. Social rank was everything to George Percy. How could this help a struggling colony on the brink of starvation?

Regardless of the weather or work to be done, Percy insisted on wearing a stiff-collared suit, hat with a gold band, and ribbon-laced shoes. This fussiness did nothing to help George Percy negotiate with Chief Powhatan.

The Native American leader had assumed the English would eventually die out because their colony always seemed on the brink of disaster. However, every several months, another ship arrived, depositing more white people on Virginia's shores.

Chief Powhatan decided the time had come to dislodge the English from their perch in America.

In the fall of 1609, he declared that any colonist or livestock found outside Jamestown fort would be killed. Hundreds of panicked settlers crowded inside the palisade. The fort became a coffin and Jane Doe was locked inside.

A monstrous hunger was set loose in the fort that winter. By November, all food stores were gone, and people consumed anything remotely edible. Seven horses had arrived with the resupply fleet. They were the first to go.

Next, the dogs were eaten, then cats, rats, and mice.

Hunger makes the best seasoning—people ate snakes and other "vermin." Toadstools and fungi that grew in the dark, damp corners of the fort were gobbled up.

When every living thing had been eaten, the colonists gnawed on their leather shoes and boots. They boiled the starched collars of their shirts to make a gluey porridge. But bellies remained achingly empty and people became desperate.

There was plenty of meat nearby. People were dying in droves, their bodies hastily buried in graves just outside the palisade. Jamestown was a society in chaos, and rules can mean little to people dying of hunger.

Those graves held something that could feed them, and some settlers decided to dig.

In the spring of 2012, archaeologists excavating the site of Jamestown's fort discovered a cellar. Clay pots and a brick oven emerged from the ground first. The diggers unearthed a garbage pit containing horse and dog bones. One morning, a worker scraping in the dirt uncovered a human jaw.

Slowly but surely, Jane Doe rose from her final resting place. Modern science has coaxed out the story her remains have been waiting centuries to tell.

"I was 14 years old when I died," whisper Jane Doe's shin bones. "I came from the southern coast of England," mumble her teeth.

Bones fill in more gaps from Jane Doe's life. A high concentration of nitrogen is evidence that she ate a lot of meat. This means she was probably the servant of a wealthy gentleman. Only the rich could afford regular meals of meat.

More evidence indicated that Jane Doe ate wheat and barley, grains found only in Europe during the seventeenth century. This proves she did not live more than a few months in America, where corn was the only available grain.

Jane's thin bones show signs of malnutrition and disease. These conditions were what killed her.

Jane did not rest peacefully after death, but that part of the story is told by her skull. On Jane Doe's forehead, there are a series of closely spaced, parallel chop marks.

"After I died," Jane Doe's skull shouts, "someone took me from my grave and butchered me!"

The evenness of the marks on the forehead prove she was dead when the carving began. A living person would have struggled, sending the butcher's knife in every direction.

But whoever tried to cut open Jane Doe's face could not do it.

The chop marks were not strong enough to break through bone. The person wielding the knife must have struggled between hunger and self-loathing as he stared down at her youthful face.

So, the butcher flipped the girl over. Jane Doe was struck repeatedly on the back of the head with enough force to split her skull in two. Then, her left temple was pried open, the hungry settler seeking her brain. A rich source of nutrients, animal brain was a common dish in the seventeenth century.

Jane Doe's tongue and the tissue of her throat and cheeks were also removed. Tiny scrape marks along her lower jaw reveal that someone was determined to get every last morsel of meat from Jane's bones.

Colonial documents reveal that there are probably other bones buried in Jamestown's fort with similar stories to tell. In 1624, a group of settlers admitted to eating "those things which nature most [hated], the flesh and excrements of man. . . ."

The minutes of the Virginia General Assembly that same year noted that during the "Starving Time," "many . . . fed on the corpses of dead men." One Native American who had been killed was buried, and three days later, his body was dug up and "boiled and stewed with roots and herbs" and "wholly devoured."

Famine played havoc with peoples' minds.

Weak settlers grew jealous at the sight of those with more flesh on their bones. They lay in wait for their meatier countrymen, "threaten[ing] to kill and eat them."

One man did more than threaten. Henry Collins! murdered his pregnant wife and tossed the unborn child into the river. Then he cut up and salted his wife's body parts and hid the pieces in his cabin.

When someone reported the wife missing, authorities searched Henry Collins's house and found the woman's "mangled body." George Percy ordered the man hung by his thumbs with weights attached to his feet until the man confessed. Then, Henry Collins was burned to death.

Jamestown's descent into darkness was eventually revealed to the outside world.

In the spring of 1610, a small ship sailed up the river and docked at Jamestown. The people who disembarked were the passengers of the ill-fated *Sea Venture*.

The flagship had not been lost during the hurricane after all. Crippled by a leaky hull, the vessel made it to Bermuda.

For the next 10 months, the 150 surviving passengers and crew were castaways on the island. Lucky for them, Bermuda fed them far better than Jamestown fed their countrymen. On Bermuda, they fished for giant sea turtles and feasted on crabs, oysters, wild boar, and fresh fruit.

The castaways built a new ship out of lumber salvaged from the *Sea Venture*, and on May 10, 1610, they escaped the devilish reefs surrounding Bermuda and sailed through 700 miles of ocean to Jamestown.

When they reached shore, no one greeted them. The fort looked lifeless. Sections of the palisade had collapsed and the outer gates swung open.

The leader of the castaways, Sir Thomas Gates, rang the church bell. A few emaciated people emerged from the houses. Some were naked, others crawling on hands and knees. "We are starved!" they cried.

Out of nearly 500 colonists who had been locked in the fort the previous fall, only 60 were still alive.

Sir Gates took over command of the colony from an exhausted George Percy, who was only too happy to step down. For a few weeks, Sir Gates tried to whip Jamestown into shape.

He launched an offensive against the Native Americans.

Gates ordered his soldiers to slaughter a captive Native American queen and her children. Amputating the hands of Native American prisoners before returning them to Chief Powhatan served as a warning that Jamestown had a new leader.

Sir Gates ordered teams of men to cast fishing nets day and night. He forced settlers to clean up the fort. Rotting debris was buried. Jane Doe, along with horse and dog carcasses, was buried in a pit in a cellar, where she lay for centuries.

Despite Sir Gates' efforts, Jamestown seemed hopeless. Native Americans still attacked the fort. The fishing nets yielded little and their food would not last until the fall harvest.

Sir Gates decided there was nothing to do but "abandon the country."

Everyone crammed aboard the *Sea Venture* and prepared to sail for Newfoundland. There, they hoped to catch enough fish to feed them on the trip to England.

Anchors were raised. Soldiers fired a final salute to Virginia. The ships floated down river on the tide. It was time to go home.

Before reaching the Chesapeake Bay, the passengers spotted a longboat headed toward them. A man stood in the prow, at the front of the boat, waving at them and calling out in English.

The men in the boat carried a message from Jamestown's new royal governor, Lord De La Warr, who had been sent from London. Three ships, bearing 300 men, and a "great store of victuals, munition, and other provision," were just a few miles downriver. Everyone turned around.

Jamestown would not be abandoned after all.

Tough times continued for the next several years, but Jamestown clung stubbornly to survival. Although gold was never discovered, tobacco exports became the brown gold that finally made Jamestown a profitable colony.

Every year, more settlers arrived, including the first African slaves in 1619.

Chief Powhatan died in 1618, and his brother assumed power. Full-scale war erupted between the

Powhatan people and the colonists in 1622. British soldiers were sent to Virginia, where they cut down Native American cornfields and burned villages.

Despite Native American resistance, wave after endless wave of British settlers and soldiers proved an invasion too powerful to withstand. The descendants of Chief Powhatan continued to battle, with both guns and the law, to regain a fraction of their once-great empire.

The fort was abandoned as the colony's population grew. Williamsburg became Virginia's capital city in 1699. The peninsula was swallowed by farmland, and the James River eroded the shoreline. The fort disappeared and, as the centuries passed, people assumed it was under water.

Then, in 1994, archaeologists discovered the fort's remains. And 20 years later, they found Jane Doe.

Although Jane Doe's real name is not known, she does have a face. Scientists scanned her skull, made a three-dimensional mold of her head, and from this, a forensic artist made a model.

With high cheekbones, a narrow nose, and small chin, Jane Doe was a pretty girl.

When Bones Speak

The story of the early years of Jamestown colony is both brutal and heroic. The colony endured famine, war, and disease. Its survival led to the founding of the United States of America.

Jane Doe was silent for centuries. The people who consumed her remains did not have the strength to give her a proper burial. By throwing her bones in a trash pit, those seventeenth-century settlers left this girl where twenty-first-century scientists could find her. Through the story etched in her bones, Jane finally spoke. And what a story she had to tell.

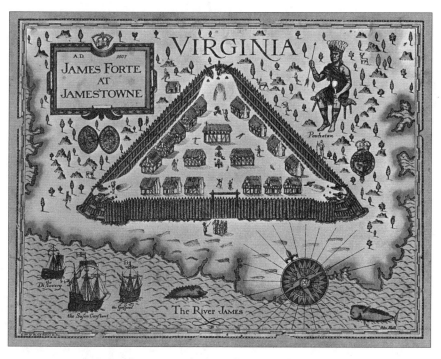

photo credit: NOAA's Historical Map & Chart Collection

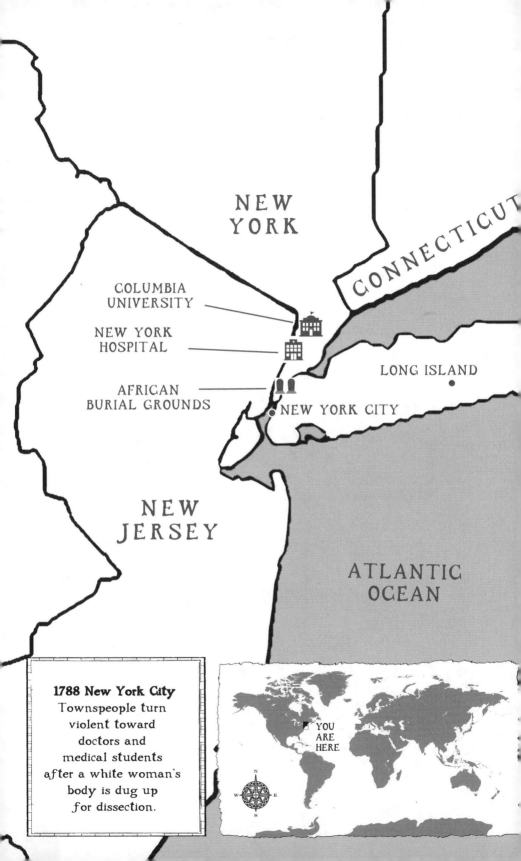

NEW
YORK

CONNECTICUT

COLUMBIA
UNIVERSITY

NEW YORK
HOSPITAL

AFRICAN
BURIAL GROUNDS

LONG ISLAND

NEW YORK CITY

NEW
JERSEY

ATLANTIC
OCEAN

1788 New York City
Townspeople turn
violent toward
doctors and
medical students
after a white woman's
body is dug up
for dissection.

YOU
ARE
HERE

1775

The American
Revolution for
independence
from England
begins

1778

The Doctors' Riot
takes place in New
York City

1789

George Washington
is elected the first
president of the
newly independent
United States

Chapter Two

The Doctors' Riot

On moonless winter nights during the 1780s,
medical students from New York City's
Columbia College worked in pairs. Dressed
in black and carrying wooden shovels over
their shoulders, they crept to the African
Burial Grounds just outside the city limits.
By the muted glow of a covered lantern,
they looked for the freshly turned soil of a
new grave. These students were not digging
for gold or precious gems. They were body
snatchers on the hunt for human remains.

In late eighteenth-century America, the medical
profession was growing and adding to its
knowledge every day. But before students could

become skilled doctors, they had to learn human anatomy. What's the best way to learn human anatomy?

By dissecting corpses.

At this time, people believed cutting up a cadaver was a sin. They feared dissection would prevent the deceased's soul from going to heaven. There was no legal way for medical students to get bodies to learn the anatomy they needed to be doctors. So, they stole them—from hospitals, morgues, and, mostly, from graveyards.

As long as body snatchers targeted African Americans and poor white people, city officials turned a blind eye to their nighttime excursions. Then, in April 1788, the grave robbers overreached. They went too far and the city exploded in the Doctors' Riot.

The job of physician was not a highly respected occupation in the eighteenth century. Columbia College was the only medical school in the whole state of New York and the requirements for becoming a doctor were pretty lax.

Boys who wanted to be doctors began college at age 15, and weren't required to earn a university degree. Taking a few classes and apprenticing under an experienced doctor was enough for a young man to call himself a doctor.

What about women who wanted to be doctors? In the eighteenth century, that wasn't even an option.

Students who weren't interested in getting their degree from Columbia enrolled in classes taught by Richard Bayley at New York Hospital. Bayley had

John Hunter
Painted by John Jackson in 1813, after an
original by Sir Joshua Reynolds in 1786

trained in London under John Hunter, one of the most distinguished scientists and surgeons of the eighteenth century.

In an age when doctors still bled and blistered patients to cure whatever ailed them, Hunter preferred to operate. At the age of 21, he became an assistant in his older brother's anatomy school. During the course of his career, Hunter admitted he had carved up "some thousands" of human bodies.

Richard Bayley learned how to be a surgeon from John Hunter. At lectures held six nights a week, Bayley took notes and studied pickled organs, dried muscles, and bone samples.

Every student at Hunter's school was guaranteed his own personal corpse to practice on. Bayley unraveled guts and squeezed lungs and weighed the human heart. He spent hours up to his elbows inside carcasses.

In 1786, Bayley began teaching an introductory class in anatomy and surgery at New York Hospital. Along with his surgical skills, Bayley also brought knowledge of the darker side of the medical profession that he had learned from John Hunter.

The art of body snatching.

The Doctors' Riot

In both the United States and Great Britain, there was no legal way for doctors to obtain corpses for dissection. So, they stole dead bodies from the ground.

A class of professional grave robbers eventually arose in England. These rival gangs were called resurrectionists because of how they could raise the dead. Some teams of resurrectionists could unearth a body in just 15 minutes.

At the height of the body-snatching era, a team would excavate as many as 10 bodies a night, about 300 a year.

Grave diggers, night watchmen, and church employees often worked with the resurrectionists. These people told the resurrectionists when a fresh body had been buried.

Before this system developed, John Hunter himself was in charge of getting bodies for his classrooms. He led crews of daredevil students on graveyard raids. If Richard Bayley did not go on one of these raids himself, he most certainly was aware of them.

So, when Bayley returned to the United States and needed corpses, he knew how to get them.

In New York City, medical students did the dirty work. Whether Bayley ordered his teenage students to go on graveyard runs is unknown, but without bodies, the young men could not perform dissections. Without dissections, they could not become doctors.

In the eyes of the medical community, stealing corpses was a necessary evil.

Technically, body snatching was a crime in New York. But as long as students confined their nightly raids to the African Burial Ground, no one in power tried to stop them.

———◆———

Collect Pond was a five-acre lake outside New York City. Once a lovely spot, by the late eighteenth century, the lake had become a cesspool. Slaughterhouses and tanneries surrounded the lake and dumped their waste into the water.

On a patch of land in a wooded area near Collect Pond was the African Burial Ground. It was the only site where black people were permitted to bury their dead.

At the time, New York City had a population of 25,000 people. Of these, about 15 percent were African Americans, most of them slaves.

The Dutch had brought 11 kidnapped Africans to New Amsterdam in 1626 to help them build the settlement that later became New York. These slaves built a fort, ships, and roads. As the colony grew, so did its slave population. When the American Revolution began in 1776, New York had more slaves than any other colony except South Carolina.

Slaves had no rights, in life or in death.

Forbidden by law to gather in groups of more than three, slaves risked punishment by attending funerals at the burial ground. Often unable to afford a casket, they wrapped their friends and family in shrouds and lowered them into the ground. As years went by, people were buried on top of each other.

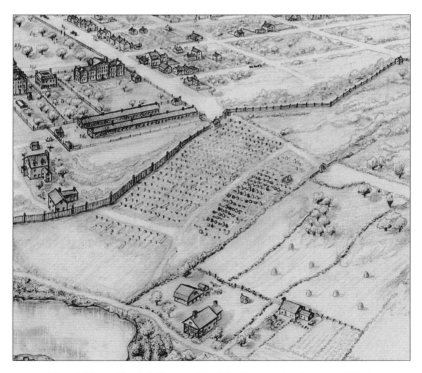

The African Burial Ground in Manhattan in the late 1700s

New Yorkers, both black and white, knew that body snatchers wanted corpses. The fresher the better. Decay begins at the moment of death and embalming would not be common practice for decades.

Medical students packed cadavers in snow and pickled organs in wine or whiskey to preserve them. However, specimens still rotted quickly. Students tried to snatch bodies as soon as they were laid in the ground.

To protect their dead, the rich might hire a night watchman to guard the grave for a week or two. They might also purchase an iron cage in which to place the coffin.

Free blacks, who were generally poor, and slaves, who owned nothing, could not afford these kinds of security measures. This was why the dissection tables at New York Hospital and Columbia College were lined with black bodies.

African Americans tried to bring the force of law down on the body snatchers. On February 14, 1787, free and enslaved blacks petitioned the New York Common Council to act.

They told city leaders that medical students under "cover of the Night" went to the burial ground to "dig up the bodies of our deceased friends and relatives" only to "mangle their flesh out of a wanton curiosity, and then expose it to Beasts and Birds."

But the council did nothing.

One New Yorker wrote that because the only people being dissected were "productions of Africa . . . surely no person can object."

After all, science must make progress.

———◆———

The pace of the graveyard thefts increased. The body snatchers grew careless, no longer bothering to cover their tracks.

On February 16, 1788, someone wrote a letter to the *New York Daily Advertiser* complaining that "few blacks are buried whose bodies are permitted to remain in the grave." The article described how students in the middle of pilfering a grave had gotten spooked and run off, leaving exposed corpses. Pigs came along and had "been devouring the entrails and flesh of women."

The medical students had also gotten sloppy about how they disposed of body parts after a dissection. The same letter writer complained that "human flesh has been taken up along the docks . . . sewed up in bags."

Many citizens were revolted by these gory reports, but no official action was taken to stop it. City leaders chose not to interfere with science as long as it was only African-American bodies and the occasional unclaimed corpse of a poor white person were being stolen.

Then, the students crossed a line. On February 21, a newspaper reported that a woman's body had been stolen from the Trinity Church graveyard.

Wealthy white people attended Trinity Church.

New York was in an uproar. The church rector offered $100 for information leading to the arrest of the body snatchers. This was a huge sum of money in 1788.

Letters poured into the *Daily Advertiser* against the medical students. One letter, penned by a "Student of Physic," warned the body snatchers that "lives may be the forfeit . . . should they dare persist."

But the students did persist.

A prank gone bad might be what sparked the Doctors' Riot of 1788. On April 13, a group of kids was playing under a window of New York Hospital where Richard Bayley's anatomy classes were being

New York Hospital

held. A teenage student named John Hicks was dissecting an arm. He heard the kids below and leaned out the window.

He held up the bloody arm and waved it. "This is your mother's arm," he called. "I just dug it up."

Unfortunately, the mother of one of the boys had recently died. The boy ran to the site where his father, a mason, was working. When the boy repeated what Hicks had said, his father was horrified. He went to the graveyard and exhumed his wife's coffin.

It was empty.

Soon, a gang of the father's fellow masons, armed with rage and hammers and chisels, was marching toward the hospital. Curious New Yorkers fell into step and the mob swelled. Anger jumped from one man to the next and people cried out for vengeance against the body snatchers.

The medical students inside the hospital heard the pounding feet of the oncoming mob. Perhaps John Hicks looked out the window in horror as he realized what his tasteless joke had unleashed.

As the enraged masons poured into the hospital's front door, most of the medical students flowed out the side exits. Dr. Wright Post, Richard Bayley's student, and four senior medical students stayed behind to protect the collection of anatomical specimens that had taken Bayley years to collect.

But these students were a poor match for the angry mob. The sight of skeletons dangling from ceilings and jars of pickled organs lining the shelves inflamed the crowd and made the masons furious.

One observer wrote, "There was a terrible rattling of bones, as they tore down and smashed every anatomical specimen they could lay their hands on."

The sight that greeted the mob when it reached the dissection rooms was the stuff of nightmares. Body parts boiled in a kettle of water. Two partially dissected bodies lay sprawled out on tables. The rioters grabbed heads, arms, and legs, and thrust them out the window.

The crowd below had swelled to 2,000 people who howled at the horrible sight.

The mob carted the body parts outside, dragging along Post and the students. The human remains were tossed into a bonfire. The medical men might have been lit ablaze as well, but luckily for them, Mayor James Duane had arrived on the scene. He shoved through the crowd and ordered the sheriff to arrest Post and the students and haul them to the city jail.

Duane was not punishing the doctors—he was trying to save them. But the mob's fury was not spent yet.

Someone cried out that they must find the "odious Mr. Hicks." Bands of men fanned out across the city. When Richard Bayley got word that the rioters were going into private homes, he joined the students at the jail.

It was the safest place to be.

Meanwhile, John Hicks had fled to the home of John Cochrane. Cochrane was a retired doctor and highly respected, so perhaps Hicks thought no one would try to search his home.

Hicks was wrong.

Rioters forced their way through Cochrane's door and searched the house from basement to attic. One of the men popped open a hatch to the roof and slowly scanned the roof.

But the hunter did not spot his prey. Hicks squatted, trembling and sweating, behind the chimney on the roof of the neighboring house.

As darkness fell, the crowd dispersed. City officials and the medical community breathed a sigh of relief, convinced they had dodged a bullet. But all night long, conversations continued among citizens. Men gathered in taverns and parlors and on street corners.

The body snatchers must pay for their crimes.

The next morning, some 400 angry men gathered in the yard of New York Hospital.

"There must be more bodies!" someone cried.

"Let's search the building again," said another.

"The physics' houses, too," shouted a third.

The commotion brought more people out on the street and the mob grew larger than it had been the day before. The tension in the city was thick and city officials were terrified.

The Doctors' Riot

Governor George Clinton and Mayor Duane joined Baron von Steuben, the German general who had aided George Washington during the Revolutionary War. They needed to act.

Together with other prominent citizens, the men marched up Broadway Avenue to the hospital steps. They pleaded with the crowd to have some self respect and go home. Law-abiding citizens do not use violence.

They promised that a full investigation into the grave robberies would be conducted and the guilty would be punished.

Some people were satisfied with these promises, but not many. The mob still swelled in anger. The officials watched helplessly as the crowd of thousands headed toward Columbia College.

Alexander Hamilton stood on the steps of Columbia. He was a graduate of the college, General Washington's right-hand man during the American Revolution, and an accomplished lawyer.

Hamilton was confident he could stop this mob.

He held up both hands and in a booming voice ordered the crowd to go home. The rioters shoved right past him and flowed into the building.

No place was off limits. The rioters searched the college museum, chapel, library, anatomical theater, and even students' bedrooms. No body parts were found.

Smart students had hidden their specimens the night before.

Its thirst for justice still unquenched, the crowd targeted the houses of physicians next. Many members of the medical profession had escaped the city the night before.

Those left behind were forced to hide.

One poor man was beaten simply because he was wearing black, the color of the robes worn by doctors and students. But when they did not find hordes of corpses stashed in anyone's closet, the group slowly broke up.

Mayor Duane barely had time to congratulate himself on narrowly averting a catastrophe when the mob reassembled in the afternoon. This time, people gathered around the city jail, and the mood had turned even uglier. The building was sheltering doctors and medical students, and the mob wanted their blood.

"Bring out your doctors!" people cried.

"We'll tear the jail down if you don't turn over the doctors!"

Inside the building, Bayley, Post, and the students must have trembled at the angry roar. They barricaded the doors and windows and armed themselves with whatever they could find.

The Doctors' Riot

The governor, mayor, and other leaders returned
to the scene. Again, their pleas for order and reason
fell on deaf ears.

"Bring out your doctors!" the mob bellowed.

Fearing someone was going to get killed any
second, Governor Clinton summoned the militia.
At 3:00 in the afternoon, a small detachment of
soldiers marched up the street. The crowd fell
quiet and parted to let the soldiers advance. But as
the militia moved through the throng of people, a
shower of dirt, stones, and catcalls followed them.

The soldiers must have been under orders to hold
their fire because they just marched away—to the
delight of the jeering crowd.

A little while later, a second group of militia
arrived on the scene. The crowd immediately burst
into laughter at the sight of the 12 men. With insults
and taunts, the mob rushed the soldiers, snatching
away their muskets. They quickly broke the
weapons into pieces on the pavement. This open
act of resistance ignited the rioters.

"To the jail!" someone cried.

"To the jail!" the mob echoed.

A sea of people rushed the building. Men
rammed their shoulders into the doors. Since the

people inside the jail had secured all entrances with bolts and bars, all the rioters got were sore shoulders.

However, there were no bars on the windows. The rioters picked up rocks and bricks off the ground and hurled them at the glass. Windows smashed, but the medical students inside the jail crawled over the broken glass and beat back the intruders with nightsticks and chair legs.

The rioters fell back, but only for the moment. Soon, a shower of stones and bricks flew through the air, forcing the students to duck and dodge. A couple of rioters threw themselves into the window openings.

Now, the rocks and bricks the rioters had just thrown were used against them. Students picked up the projectiles and slammed them into any head that popped into a window.

Only one man managed to climb all the way into the jail, and a guard shot and killed him.

The governor ordered up more militia. This time a "large body . . . under an experienced officer" marched up Broadway, the soldiers' bayonets gleaming in the starlight. A cry of defiance went up among the rioters and they hurled themselves at the oncoming troops.

Seconds earlier, General von Steuben had been cautioning Governor Clinton not to let the soldiers fire on the crowd. Suddenly, a rock struck von Steuben in the forehead.

That did it. All sympathy he felt for the citizens vanished. As he fell, von Steuben yelled, "Fire, Governor, fire!"

The commander of the militia cried out, "Ready. Aim. Fire!" The flash of musket fire lit up the dim night. The scowling mob, battered jail door, and panicked faces of the people peering out the jail windows were all illuminated for one brief second.

The rioters were struck dumb. All day, city officials had used persuasion, not force to try to calm the situation. Now, bullets were flying. No one moved.

The officer ordered another volley and musket balls slammed into the crowd with deadly force. That woke the people up. Rioters ran in every direction. Soon, the only people left in the jail yard were the dead, the wounded, and the militia. The soldiers stood guard all night, but the violence was over.

An uneasy calm descended around the hospital, as well, the silence broken only by the moans of the wounded who had been brought there.

◆

The next day, rumors spread door to door through New York City. The faster the rumors raced, the higher the death toll of the day.

At least three soldiers were killed. The number of rioters who died varies between three and 20, depending on whose account is believed.

The militia stood guard around the hospital for several days. Groups of men clustered on blood-stained street corners, cursing both the militia and the medical profession.

The violence had ended, but goodwill did not return. Medical students stayed away from the city for several weeks. New York newspapers stopped running ads for doctors and medical classes. People organized cemetery patrols called "Dead Guard Men" to watch the graveyards at night.

Richard Bayley published a notice in the paper insisting that he had never robbed a cemetery in the city nor asked anyone else to rob a grave for him.

The key phrase he used was "in the city."

The African Burial Ground was outside New York City limits.

A grand jury investigated the causes of the riot. Some students were charged, but no one was ever convicted for body snatching. John Hicks never appeared in court. He eventually completed his medical training and became a surgeon, but died in a yellow fever epidemic in 1798.

The Doctors' Riot of 1788 convinced political leaders to give doctors one legal source of cadavers. In 1789, the New York legislature passed a law to prevent the "odious practice . . . of digging up the dead." The law made grave robbery illegal and declared that violators would be publicly whipped, fined, and imprisoned.

But the law also allowed medical schools to dissect criminals who had been executed for murder, arson, and burglary. Lawmakers were trying to help scientific progress without offending public morals.

However, the number of people executed each year was tiny compared to the number of bodies medical schools needed for dissection. So, the body snatching continued.

The riot just taught students to cover their tracks a little better.

Finally, in 1854, New York legalized the dissection of unclaimed bodies left abandoned in city morgues. This change was sorely needed because by that time, body snatchers were stealing about 700 bodies a year in New York City.

Tomb Raiders

Today, medical students continue to dissect cadavers in New York City medical schools and in medical schools across the country. These bodies are donated to science by the people themselves upon their death.

Many consider it an honor to give their bodies to medical schools to further science and medical training. They willingly do so.

As New York City grew, Collect Pond was filled in and the African Burial Ground was covered over by roads. But in 1991, construction workers there discovered bones. Lots of bones. Ultimately, archaeologists sent 419 skeletons to Howard University for analysis.

Today, the African Burial Ground is a national monument. A black marble wall marks the place where African Americans were laid to rest centuries before. The wall resembles a tombstone, but is as tall as the sail of a slave ship.

Adjacent to the marble wall are seven grassy mounds and underneath these lie seven burial crypts. Unlike their brothers and sisters whose remains were stolen by body snatchers, the 419 dead discovered in 1991 were reburied with honor.

The wall carries this epitaph:

For all those who were lost
For all those who were stolen
For all those who were left behind
For all those who were not forgotten.

photo credit: National Park Service

WISCONSIN

MICHIGAN

IOWA

CHICAGO

INDIANA

SPRINGFIELD

ILLINOIS

MISSOURI

KENTUCKY

1. 1865 Washington, DC
Abraham Lincoln is killed
by John Wilkes Booth
at Ford's Theater.

2. 1876 Chicago, Illinois
Counterfeiters plot to
steal President Lincoln's
corpse from its tomb
in Springfield, Illinois,
and hold it for ransom.

YOU
ARE
HERE

N
W   E
S

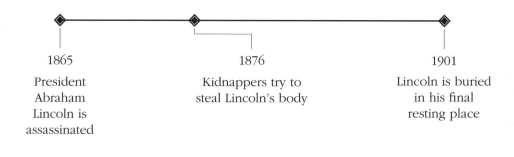

1865
President
Abraham
Lincoln is
assassinated

1876
Kidnappers try to
steal Lincoln's body

1901
Lincoln is buried
in his final
resting place

Chapter Three

Corpse for Ransom

A bust of Abraham Lincoln sat behind the
bar at a saloon on Chicago's west side called
the Hub. By 1876, Lincoln had been dead
for 11 years, but the sixteenth president kept
watch as customers swigged beer and spit
tobacco on the sawdust-covered floor.

One August afternoon, James Kennally walked into
the Hub. The tall, light-eyed man, better known
as "Big Jim," co-owned the saloon with bartender
Terrance Mullen. The mustachioed Mullen managed
the tavern while Kennally oversaw the more
profitable side of the business—counterfeiting.

Kennally exchanged a look with Mullen and
disappeared into one of the back rooms of the Hub.
Mullen followed him. Minutes later, two more men,
Jack Hughes and Herbert Nelson, joined the meeting.

These counterfeiters, called coney men, ran a smooth criminal operation. Kennally took orders from gangs for a certain quantity of fake money. He paid engravers and printers to fill these orders. When the counterfeit money was ready, Herbert Nelson and other distributors transported the bills to a pickup location.

Mullen, also a distributor, worked right from the saloon. He slipped rolls of bills to men called "shovers" along with their mugs of beer or shots of whiskey. Shovers took the money and went shopping.

Jack Hughes was a shover.

After getting the counterfeit cash from Mullen, Hughes pocketed one fake bill and gave the rest to a teenage boy who was his accomplice. Hughes would enter a store alone and make a low-cost purchase with the phony bill. If the shopkeeper accepted the bill, Hughes pocketed the change. Then, Hughes and his sidekick proceeded to the next store.

After a few hours, Hughes had a pocket full of genuine cash. If the store owner spotted the fake bill, Hughes put on a show, apologizing and complaining about how counterfeiters were robbing people blind. Then, he paid for his purchase with real money and tried again at the next store.

Pretty clever, right?

Corpse for Ransom

◆

The Civil War had begun in 1861 and launched the golden age of counterfeiting. Prior to the war, the federal government only coined gold and silver money, not paper bills. Banks printed their own form of currency, called banknotes. Each bank designed its own note, which made creating forgeries of them a real challenge for counterfeiters.

When the war began, the federal government needed more cash, but did not have enough supplies of gold and silver to make enough coins. So, in 1862, the U.S. Congress authorized the government to print $150 million dollars' worth of paper money that would be recognized as legal everywhere.

Counterfeiters were thrilled!

Engravers needed to make only a few different styles of metal plates for the different denominations. Printers could make thousands of copies of bills and shovers could use them in stores across the country, getting real money as change.

However, counterfeiting depended on the skill of the engraver. If the bills did not look genuine, the coney men would get busted.

The best engraver in the Midwest was a man named Benjamin Boyd, and he worked for Big Jim Kennally.

When the Civil War ended in April 1865, the federal government began to crack down on counterfeiters. The U.S. Treasury Department created a new agency whose sole function was to nab counterfeiters—the Secret Service.

One of Chicago's most hardworking Secret Service agents was Patrick Tyrrell. On October 21, 1875, Tyrrell raided Benjamin Boyd's house and confiscated fake money and counterfeiting tools. Boyd was sentenced to 10 years in the federal penitentiary in Joliet, Illinois.

With Boyd behind bars, Kennally's criminal network began to feel the pinch. Their supply of quality counterfeit money ran low. Kennally decided his only recourse was to get Boyd out of prison. This was the reason for the August meeting at the Hub.

From his shelf behind the bar, Lincoln's bust could not eavesdrop on the men. If he could have followed the four men into the back room, Lincoln would have been shocked at what he heard.

"We'll break into Lincoln's tomb in Springfield, Illinois," Kennally said. "Nab his body and hold it for ransom. If the feds want old Abe back, they'll have to set Boyd free first."

There must have been a stunned silence as the other men stared at Kennally in shock.

"We're coney men, not body snatchers," one of them finally said.

"It will be easy," Kennally assured them.

Oak Ridge Cemetery was two miles from Springfield. No watchman guarded the monument that held Lincoln's coffin, and only one padlock secured the door. Kennally wanted the men to transport Lincoln's casket to the sand dunes on the Indiana side of Lake Michigan, where they would bury it in the sand while Kennally sent the governor the ransom note.

Mullen, Hughes, and Nelson exchanged skeptical looks. The Indiana sand dunes were 220 miles from Springfield. The journey would take days.

Then, Kennally sweetened the pot. "We'll tell the feds we also want $200,000. In cash."

That did the trick. The men agreed to kidnap Lincoln's corpse.

The evening of April 14, 1865, President Abraham Lincoln had reason to enjoy a night on the town. For

The president's box at Ford's Theater
photo credit: Library of Congress

four long years, Lincoln had struggled to keep the United States from falling apart as the Civil War raged between the North and South.

Now, the bloody conflict was over. Lincoln and his wife, Mary, planned to celebrate that evening by attending a show at Ford's Theater in Washington, DC. A comedy was playing, and Lincoln needed a good laugh.

That evening, the Lincolns and two friends entered a private box above the right side of the stage. Noting the president's arrival, the band played "Hail to the Chief."

Lincoln bowed and took his seat.

Police officer John Parker stood guard outside the door to the presidential box, but at intermission, he abandoned his post and went to the nearby Star Saloon for a drink. Actor and Confederate sympathizer John Wilkes Booth had been at the same bar earlier, nursing his hatred for Lincoln. Booth was bitter because the South had lost the Civil War.

Booth entered Ford's Theater around 10 p.m. The presidential box remained unguarded. Booth opened the door and slipped inside unseen. The actor pointed his pistol at the back of Lincoln's head and waited for a punchline.

When the audience exploded into laughter, Booth pulled the trigger.

Lincoln slumped forward in his chair. Mary screamed and reached for him. Booth yelled, "Thus always to tyrants," and leapt over the box. The spur on his boot caught in a flag and Booth crashed on the stage, breaking his left shin. The audience thought the action was part of the play and just sat there as Booth escaped through a back door.

Then Mary Lincoln yelled, "They have shot the president!" An unconscious Lincoln was carried across the street to a boardinghouse. The assassin's bullet had ripped a path through the left side of Lincoln's brain. Recovery was impossible.

Abraham Lincoln died at 7:22 a.m. on April 15, 1965.

◆

Later that day, undertaker Henry Cattrell leaned over President Lincoln's body in a guest room of the White House. He sliced into the president's upper thigh and pumped in a fluid containing zinc chloride. Lincoln's corpse slowly turned white as marble. Cattrell shaved Lincoln, arched his eyebrows, and molded his lips into a slight smile. The president was dressed in a black suit, bow tie, and white gloves.

Mary Lincoln had decided to bury her husband in Oak Ridge Cemetery in Springfield, Illinois. Shaded by trees and bordering a small creek, Oak Ridge offered the peace Lincoln had craved at the end of his life. The president's body was housed in a temporary vault cut into a hillside while his permanent tomb was constructed by the National Lincoln Monument Association.

In 1871, the Lincoln Monument was finally ready. An 85-foot-tall obelisk capped the structure. A spiral iron staircase inside the obelisk led visitors to a terrace that offered a clear view of the grounds.

Below the terrace was Memorial Hall, which contained a small museum of Lincoln memorabilia.

NATIONAL LINCOLN MONUMENT,

photo credit: Mead, Larkin G., Strobridge & Co. Lith., lithographer

The tomb chamber, called the catacomb, was accessible through a door on the other side of the building.

This room contained five crypts, for Lincoln's sons and his wife. Lincoln's body was rested in a cocoon of coffins—an airtight lead coffin inside a red cedar casket inside a white marble sarcophagus. The magnificent sarcophagus dominated the room. A double door guarded the catacomb, along with a wooden outer door and a padlocked iron grate.

The monument was open for tours led by John Carroll Power, the custodian of the building. Power led people through Memorial Hall, but they could view Lincoln's sarcophagus only through the iron grilled door.

Only Power had a key to the catacomb. The president's tomb was sacred and not to be disturbed.

That was about to change.

———◆———

In the summer of 1876, the Chicago police nabbed Jack Hughes's teenage accomplice with a pocket full of fake cash. To cut a deal, the boy offered to squeal on Jack Hughes. The Chicago police notified Patrick Tyrrell that they had information on a counterfeiter.

Patrick Tyrrell had heard of Jack Hughes. A year earlier, the man had been arrested for trying to pass fake five dollar bills, but he had jumped bail and never been caught.

When Tyrrell interrogated the teenager, he learned that Hughes hung out at the Hub. Here was his chance. Tyrrell decided to bust Hughes and the ring of counterfeiters.

To do this, Tyrrell needed a good roper.

A roper was a paid informant, usually an ex-con. A roper gained the trust of criminals and, for a fee, fed the cops inside information about how the criminal enterprise worked. The life of a roper was dangerous. Nobody likes a snitch.

The roper Tyrrell chose was Lewis Swegles, a horse thief who had served prison time in Wisconsin. While behind bars, Swegles had met many coney men. Now, he was living in Chicago and trying to stay out of trouble. For five dollars a day, Swegles agreed to be Tyrrell's roper.

The timing was perfect. Kennally had ordered Mullen and Hughes to find a fourth man for the kidnapping job. One day, Lewis Swegles entered the Hub and began bragging about his days as a horse thief.

Mullen and Hughes paid attention. Gradually, Swegles earned their friendship, and in October, they pulled Swegles aside.

"Do you want to make some quick money?" they asked.

"It depends on the job," Swegles said. He figured it would involve counterfeiting.

A rich businessman had just died in Kenosha, Wisconsin, Mullen and Hughes explained. They wanted to snatch the man's body and hold it for ransom. "Do you want in?" they asked.

Swegles must have been shocked, but he played it cool.

"Before I decide," he said, "let me look up the penalty for grave robbing in Wisconsin."

Swegles decided the coneys were testing him, and a couple days later he turned down the job. Mullen and Hughes were not upset. Swegles was right—they had been testing him.

There was no dead rich man in Kenosha. The coney men wanted to see if Swegles could keep secrets. They listened for any rumors of the kidnapping plot, but Swegles kept his mouth shut. Mullen and Hughes decided he was their man.

One night, they took Swegles into one of the Hub's back rooms.

"Forget the Wisconsin job," Mullen said. "We're going to do a body-snatching, but we're after something much bigger.

Swegles listened in stunned silence as the men laid out the plan. Take the train to Springfield. Break into the Lincoln Monument and steal Lincoln's corpse. Drive to the Indiana sand dunes and bury the corpse in the sand. Contact the governor of Illinois and demand the release of Benjamin Boyd and $200,000.

The men waited for Swegles's answer. The roper's brain raced for the right response to convince the men he was one of them. "I'm the body snatcher of Chicago!" he crowed.

Shortly after this, Herbert Nelson got cold feet and backed out of the job. However, Swegles had a solution. Since Lincoln was lying in a marble sarcophagus, they needed a cracksman, a specialist at breaking through tough surfaces. Swegles told the coneys he had a friend named Billy Brown who could do the job.

In reality, there was no Billy Brown. Swegles's friend was actually Bill Neely, an honest bricklayer, willing to play the role of cracksman. Mullen and Hughes invited Brown to join the team.

The kidnapping crew was in place.

◆

As the crooks debated when to make their move, the nation found itself embroiled in an intense battle for the presidency. The Republican governor of Ohio, Rutherford B. Hayes, was pitted against Samuel Tilden, the Democratic governor of New York. The race was neck and neck.

Election Day was November 7. The people of Springfield would go to the polls and wait anxiously for election results. No one would be visiting Oak Ridge Cemetery. On November 6, Mullen decided the evening of election day would be "a damned elegant time to [kidnap Lincoln]."

When Swegles gave him the word, Patrick Tyrrell flew into action. He informed John Carroll Power, the custodian of the Lincoln Monument, of the plot. He also recruited four men to help him—the former Chicago chief of police, Elmer Washburn; John McDonald, a Secret Service agent stationed near Springfield; and two private detectives from the Pinkerton Detective Agency, John McGinn and George Hay.

By 8 p.m. that night, Tyrrell, McGinn, and Hay were hiding in the shadows of Chicago's central train station. The train would depart for Springfield at 9 p.m.

Minutes ticked by, but the coney men were nowhere in sight. Worry ran like a spider up Tyrrell's spine. Had his roper double-crossed him?

At 9 p.m. the whistle blew, the wheels began to churn, and the train chugged slowly down the tracks. Suddenly, four men dashed out of the station and leaped on the first car. Tyrrell beckoned to his team and they jumped into the last car just as the train left the station.

The game was on.

At 6 a.m. on November 7, the train reached Springfield. Unknown to Mullen and Hughes, Billy Brown, aka Bill Neely, had gotten off the train in the middle of the night. Swegles told the coney men that Brown was asleep in another car. The train was not scheduled to depart for some time, and Swegles said he would return to the station and wake Brown up later. The coney men checked into the St. Charles House hotel, unaware that the detectives were staying at a hotel only two blocks away.

While Mullen and Hughes ordered breakfast, Swegles said he would go wake Brown so he could find a wagon and horse team to hire as their getaway vehicle. As soon as Swegles was out of sight of the St. Charles House, he doubled back to the detectives' hotel and met with Tyrrell to finalize their plan to trap the thieves.

Both cops and crooks toured Lincoln's tomb that day. In the morning, John Carroll Power showed Tyrrell the catacomb where Lincoln's sarcophagus sat in front of a brick wall.

Tyrrell wanted to know what was behind the wall. Power took Tyrrell inside Memorial Hall and through a door into a labyrinth. The space was a maze of thick walls and piles of lumber lay everywhere. The damp air smelled like rotting wood. Water seeped through the stone ceiling and pooled on the floor.

Tyrrell stood by the brick wall and Power returned to the catacomb and rapped on the wall from the other side. Tyrrell heard him perfectly. As long as the detectives were completely silent, they could hide in the labyrinth and listen to the coney men until the time was right to spring their trap.

That afternoon, Hughes and Swegles also toured Lincoln's Monument. Power did not show them the labyrinth.

The skies were gray and rain threatened all day. Elmer Washburn and Secret Service agent John McDonald arrived on the five o'clock train with a journalist named Percy English in tow. English would record the night's events for the *Chicago Tribune*.

When darkness fell, the detectives hired a carriage to drive them to the cemetery. John Carroll Power was waiting for them. Once inside Memorial Hall, Power locked the door behind them and everyone extinguished their lanterns.

"The darkness could almost be felt," Power later wrote.

The men held hands as Power blindly led the way into the labyrinth. When he had reached a spot where no light would be visible from outside, he lit a lantern. Then, Tyrrell placed a series of lanterns along the narrow corridor leading to the brick wall. He ordered Percy English to stay there.

"When you hear the criminals in the catacomb," Tyrrell said, "follow the lights back to Memorial Hall and give us the word."

English had come to Springfield to report a story, but now he was part of the story.

The rest of the team moved into position, their heels echoing on the marble floor of the hall. This operation required complete silence. Tyrrell ordered the team to remove their boots. Then, he took his spot by the outside door and settled in to wait.

◆

Two hours later, Mullen, Hughes, and Swegles climbed the cemetery fence. Swegles had said Billy Brown would be waiting with a wagon and horse team near the woods outside the cemetery at 9:30. Across the dark and silent graveyard they ran toward the monument.

Mullen lit a lantern and shined it at the building. Could someone be inside? He ordered the others to take a look around. As Hughes and Swegles scouted the area, Swegles grabbed the handle of the locked door to Memorial Hall and rattled it. He flashed the light in the window but saw nothing.

"I didn't, of course, want to see anything," he said later.

Inside the hall, Tyrrell got Swegles' message. The coney men had arrived. He gestured for Power to unlock the door. Soon the detectives would need to exit this door quickly.

———◆———

The thick padlock securing the iron grate door proved tough. The saw blade broke, but Mullen managed to snap the lock with a metal file and pliers. He pushed open the door. The lantern beam spotlighted the center of the chamber, and for a moment, the thieves were mesmerized.

The marble sarcophagus gleamed in the yellow light. The word *LINCOLN* was carved on one end, sculpted oak leaves winding around the letters. Above the name was a line from Lincoln's second inaugural address. "With Malice toward None, With Charity for All."

Mullen snapped out of his trance. He picked up an axe and heaved it over his shoulder.

"Hold on!" Swegles said. Swegles jammed a crowbar under the lid. It had been sealed with only plaster, not cement. The men cracked the plaster seal, removed the sarcophagus lid, and leaned it against the wall. Inside this was a second marble lid, which they attacked with the axe and chisels.

Inside the labyrinth, Percy English heard the banging. On stockinged feet, he followed the trail of lanterns to Memorial Hall and told the others: The thieves were in the catacomb attacking Lincoln's coffin.

Tyrrell did not move. The other agents exchanged nervous glances. What was he waiting for?

Back inside the catacomb, the coney men had removed a panel at the head of the sarcophagus. Inside sat the red cedar coffin. They pulled on it as hard as they could, but the coffin was lined with two layers of lead and weighed almost 500 pounds. It slid only about a foot out of the sarcophagus and then refused to budge.

Mullen ordered Swegles to fetch Billy Brown. They needed more muscle.

Swegles left the catacomb and ran down the hill. When he reached the thicket of trees, he turned right and around the monument to Memorial Hall.

Swegles knocked lightly on the door and whispered the password. "Wash."

Tyrrell opened the door and Swegles told him the sarcophagus was open, but they could not get the coffin out. Tyrrell ordered Swegles to stay put. He motioned to Power to bring the lanterns, and then raced outside, not even pausing to put his boots back on. The team followed.

The men ran around the side of the building. Suddenly, an explosion rang out behind Tyrrell. He whipped around. Detective George Hay looked with horror at the smoking pistol in his hand. He had cocked his gun too early.

The hammer slipped and struck the cap, causing an explosion as loud as a cannon.

Tyrrell knew they had to move faster now. On lightening feet, he charged into the tomb chamber first, revolver cocked and ready. The room was as dark as pitch. "Whoever is inside better surrender!" he shouted. There was no reply.

Tyrrell yelled another warning. Silence answered him. He struck a match. The crypt was empty.

A broken saw blade lay on the floor, alongside the padlock, an axe, and two slabs of marble. One end of Lincoln's coffin rested on the floor.

Tyrrell ordered his team to search the cemetery grounds while he raced back to Memorial Hall to put on his boots. He ran up the spiral staircase to the terrace. By this time the moon had risen. Tyrrell spied two figures behind some columns and shot at them. The men fired back.

Tyrrell yelled down to Washburn, "Chief, we have the devils up here."

A few seconds later, someone called out, "Tyrrell, for God's sakes . . . is that you shooting at us?"

The figures hiding behind the columns were Detectives Hay and McGinn. The coney men had disappeared. Tyrrell's trap had turned into a fiasco.

Lincoln's corpse had not been stolen, but the counterfeiters were still on the loose, and Tyrrell was determined to nab them. On November 10, Swegles peeked through the backdoor of the Hub. Big Jim Kennally was working the bar. Swegles beckoned to him, trying to act nervous like a man on the run.

Kennally still believed Swegles was one of the gang. Swegles let out a sigh of relief. His cover had not been blown. Mullen and Hughes came out of hiding. Tyrrell was ready for them.

On November 17, at 10:30 p.m., Detective McGinn and Chicago police officer Dennis Simmons entered the Hub. Patrick Tyrrell and the former Chicago chief of police, Elmer Washburn, observed the scene through a window. Hughes was asleep in a chair and Mullen was serving drinks.

Mullen smiled pleasantly as McGinn leaned against the bar and ordered two beers. As Mullen stooped to fill the order, mugs in one hand and keg spout in the other, McGinn drew his revolver and held it against Mullin's head. "Mullen, you are my man," he said.

Simmons walked over to the sleeping Hughes. "Come along with me, my boy," he said loudly. Hughes opened his eyes to find the barrel of a gun staring back at him.

"Who are you?" Hughes asked.

The door burst open and Patrick Tyrrell entered the room.

The trial for the attempted kidnapping of Abraham Lincoln's corpse began on May 28, 1877. Mullen and Hughes claimed they had been framed, victims of a conspiracy hatched by Tyrrell and Washburn and led by Swegles, the real crook.

The jury did not buy it. Both men were convicted of conspiracy to steal Lincoln's body and attempted larceny for trying to steal the coffin. They were sentenced to one year in the federal penitentiary at Joliet.

Ironically, this is where Benjamin Boyd, the master engraver, was still serving time.

Worried about a copycat kidnapper, John Carroll Power and members of the Lincoln Monument Association moved the president's coffin to the basement of Memorial Hall on November 15, 1876.

Corpse for Ransom

In 1878, John Carroll Power recruited five strong, patriotic men to move Lincoln to the labyrinth, where they buried him in a shallow grave. The men formed a secret society called the Lincoln Guard of Honor. Their mission was to protect Abraham Lincoln's body.

A brick vault was eventually built in the original catacomb, and on April 14, 1887, Abraham Lincoln was exhumed again and reburied in this vault with Mary beside him.

During the next decade, Lincoln was relocated again. This time he was housed in a temporary vault for 18 months while a new foundation was dug.

On September 26, 1901, workers dug a 10-foot-deep hole with a steel cage inside in the floor of the catacomb. Men lowered the casket into this steel cage and poured wet concrete into the vault, slowly filling in the space around the coffin. Within hours, all that remained was a solid, unbreakable block in the catacomb floor.

Finally, 36 years after his death, the body of Abraham Lincoln could rest in peace.

MEDITERRANEAN SEA

EGYPT

● CAIRO

NILE RIVER

VALLEY OF THE KINGS ●● DEIR EL-BAHRI

● LUXOR

1871-1881

Grave robbers discover the Cache of Kings in Deir el-Bahri. They use it as a private vault until they are caught and the ancient mummies are sent to the Egyptian Museum in Cairo.

YOU ARE HERE

N W E S

1865	1871	1881
The Civil War ends in America	The Abd el-Rassul family begins looting the Deir el-Bahri grave	Authorities begin sending artifacts from Deir el-Bahri to the Egyptian Museum in Cairo

Chapter Four

The Cache of Kings

> Ancient Egyptian grave robbers rarely confessed to their heinous crimes, but one document from the twelfth century BCE survives. These thieves described how they entered a tomb and opened the royal coffins. Chains of gold laced the king's throat, and his face was covered in a gilded mask.

What thief could resist?

The robbers stripped the king and queen of every scrap of gold and silver. Then, they set fire to the couple's clothing and stole the furniture and vases from the tomb.

These men were apprehended and found guilty, but most Egyptian grave robbers escaped.

Tomb Raiders

Throughout their 3,500 years of civilization, ancient Egyptians sought immortality. They believed that after death, a person's soul split into three parts and traveled between the land of the living and the underworld.

For the soul to live forever, the dead person's body must remain intact as a kind of home that the parts of the soul could return to periodically. If the body was destroyed, the soul was forever fragmented and the person ceased to exist.

For this reason, Egyptians mummified their dead. They buried them with enough treasure to last forever in the Valley of the Kings on the west bank of the Nile River.

But ancient grave robbers were not interested in eternity. They wanted wealth in their own lifetimes.

In the Old Kingdom, pharaohs built pyramid tombs, but these stone triangles did not keep out the thieves. So, in the Middle Kingdom, the cemetery of the rich and powerful was moved to the necropolis of Thebes. This city of the dead was home to tombs, along with the priests, craft workers, and laborers who tended to the needs of the royal mummies.

The Cache of Kings

Royal tombs in Thebes
photo credit: Vyacheslav Stepanyuchenko

But some of the people who worked for a pharaoh's afterlife by day, robbed him by night. By 1550 BCE, there was scarcely a royal tomb in Thebes that had not been pillaged.

Not satisfied with stealing gold statutes, gilded furniture, or gem-studded weapons, thieves attacked the mummies themselves. They bashed skulls, cracked open chests, and ripped off limbs in search of hidden treasure.

Terrified at the thought of their splintered souls wandering for eternity, rulers abandoned the idea of building large, showy tombs. Instead, they ordered their architects to dig hidden burial chambers in the face of limestone cliffs located in the Valley of the Kings.

This lonely and forbidding valley lay west of Thebes. With its towering rock formations, natural basins, and secluded bays and ravines, the remote valley seemed ideal for secret burials.

But even this secluded gorge was not beyond the reach of highly organized gangs of thieves. They were aided by traitorous priests, bribed officials, and corrupt judges. The Valley of the Kings was systematically plundered, leaving behind a labyrinth of tunnels inside the cliffs.

Sometime between 945 and 712 BCE, a group of priests felt guilty.

They surveyed the tombs in the Valley of the Kings and found mummies whose graves had been robbed but whose bodies had survived. The priests transferred the mummies to government buildings, where they repaired and rewrapped them.

However, these priests were not just doing a good deed. Before rewrapping the monarchs, the priests stole all amulets and gold gilt that remained on the mummies and their coffins.

This was church-sanctioned grave robbery.

Still, the priests did leave the royals' bodies intact for their souls to find. They attached identity tags to new coffins and body wrappings. Then, on a dark and moonless night, the priests carried the mummies up a lonely and desolate path out of the valley.

The Cache of Kings

They moved the mummies from the Valley of the Kings to the rocky basin of Deir el-Bahri. There, in the family tomb of a high priest that had been hewn into the wall of the basin, they placed the mummies. As time passed, rain and wind erased all traces of the tomb's entrance.

This royal cache remained hidden for centuries.

One day in 1871, Ahmed Abd el-Rassul, his brother Hussein, and a thief accomplice were walking along a path on the face of a cliff in Deir el-Bahri. Below them stood the terraced temple of Queen Hatshepsut, one of ancient Egypt's two female pharaohs.

Queen Hatshepsut's burial temple
photo credit: Ijanderson977

These men were not tourists on a sightseeing stroll. They were working. The el-Rassul family did the same work as most of the people in their village of Qurnah—they were grave robbers.

In ancient times, Qurnah, the "village of robbers," sat on the edge of ancient Thebes. Mud-brick homes spilled down a rocky hillside. Black-robed women conversed in dusty streets, and children, dogs, and ducks scurried here and there. The rock under their feet was honeycombed with tombs of New Kingdom royalty.

Peasants in other villages in Egypt tilled the soil to plant vegetables. Meanwhile, the people of Qurnah cultivated a different crop—the stolen treasures of antiquity.

That day on the cliff path, Ahmed noticed a shadow behind a large boulder. He scrambled down the hillside and discovered a small opening. Ahmed tossed a rock inside and listened. Several long seconds passed before he heard a soft thud. A thrill raced through his body. This was the entrance to a shaft.

Below, a treasure might be waiting.

With shovels and chisels, the men widened the hole and dropped in a rope. Ahmed slid down the 35-foot shaft. Long minutes of silence passed. The two men on the surface grew nervous.

Suddenly, a shriek shot out of the hole. Seconds later, Ahmed scrambled up the rope. Trembling with fear, he babbled about seeing an afrit, a kind of demon that villagers believed lived in ancient tombs. Treasure forgotten, the three men ran down the cliff path.

When Ahmed and his brother got home, he told the rest of his large family what he had really seen underground. There was no afrit. When Ahmed reached the bottom of the narrow shaft, he found himself in a cramped corridor full of dark shapes. He lit a lantern and when his eyes adjusted to the light, he saw treasure.

Clusters of dusty coffins filled the room. They went down the corridor as far as Ahmed's eye could see. Royal cobras decorated some coffin lids and cartouches were painted on others. Cartouches were oblong shapes with hieroglyphics in their centers, the identity mark of kings and queens.

Ahmed had stumbled on a royal tomb.

This was the discovery of a lifetime. If the Abd el-Rassul family played their cards right, they would be set for life, but that meant keeping the tomb a secret. That's why Ahmed had screamed and lied about seeing an afrit. The villagers were superstitious and would avoid any place that might be haunted by demons.

That night, Ahmed and his older brother, Mohammed, killed a donkey and threw it down the shaft. This was a smart move. The villagers assumed the disgusting stench floating out of the ground was the angry afrit.

The Abd el-Rassul family decided to leave the treasure exactly where it was. They would remove items to sell only as the family needed money. For six years, the tomb served as a sort of mummified bank account.

Now and then, one of the men of the family would climb the wall of Deir el-Bahri at night, slide into the shaft, and pick out something of value. A papyrus scroll, a porcelain vase, a piece of cloth. He would sell this on the black market, sharing the profits with the family.

The plan worked like clockwork, until one day a savvy government official grew suspicious.

In 1881, a rich antique collector named John Francis Campbell sailed up the Nile to Luxor. This is the modern city that occupies the land where ancient Thebes once housed the Egyptian dead. Avoiding the professional antiquities dealers, Campbell visited the dark alleys and back rooms of Luxor's bazaar. He was looking for treasure on the black market.

And he found it.

Campbell purchased a papyrus in mint condition. Hiding the scroll in his trunk, he returned to Europe. There, Campbell took the papyrus to experts who declared it was a rare treasure—*the Book of the Dead of Pinedjem II*, a pharaoh from Egypt's Twenty-First Dynasty.

The experts knew that if a private collector was able to lay his hands on a valuable artifact like this, it meant he had bought it from thieves. By law, the treasures of Egypt's past were supposed to remain in the country.

The specialists sent a letter to the Egyptian Museum in Cairo. That letter eventually reached the desk of Gaston Maspero, the director-general of excavations and antiquities for Egypt. His job was to protect the remains of the country's past from grave robbers determined to sell it to the highest bidder.

Since 1858, the government had tried to stop the flood of antiquities leaving Egypt. Anyone who wanted to excavate a site had to get permission from the Antiquities Society and inspectors were permitted on the site without notice. No tomb could be entered without an inspector present. If a previously robbed tomb was excavated, the Egyptian Museum took any remaining artifacts. If an archaeologist discovered a tomb that had somehow escaped robbery, the Egyptian government laid claim to the entire site.

News of Campbell's Book of the Dead immediately aroused Director Maspero's suspicions. For the last few years, several valuable antiques had mysteriously appeared on the black market. There were rumors about who was selling these goods.

It is an Arab, said some. No, a black man, said others. A poor peasant. A rich sheikh.

No one knew for sure.

Director Maspero was determined to crack the mystery because he was certain of one thing—the valuable artifacts that had recently surfaced belonged to different kings and queens. This meant that someone had either located several tombs at once or grave robbers had stumbled upon a common tomb that held several mummies.

To help solve the case, Director Maspero enlisted the aid of someone who would not arouse the thieves' suspicions—a wealthy collector named Charles Wilbour. The collector was already known to dealers in Luxor as a man willing to pay high prices for genuine antiquities. On Maspero's request, he traveled to Luxor and wandered the bazaar, jingling the coins in his pocket and chatting up dealers.

After only a couple days, a dealer squatting in the doorway of his store beckoned Wilbour over. He had something Wilbour would want to see. The dealer led Wilbour through his crowded, dim shop into a backroom.

There, he shut the door and handed Wilbour a small statute. The collector knew enough about ancient Egypt to interpret the inscription on the statue. He was holding a 3,000-year-old piece of art from a tomb of the Twenty-First Dynasty.

Wearing a poker face, Wilbour began to haggle over price. After a lengthy bargaining session, Wilbour bought the statue. He also told the dealer that he was in the market for something bigger.

Later that day, the dealer took Wilbour to Ahmed Abd el-Rassul's house in Qurnah. Ahmed showed Wilbour a bolt of red leather stamped with the title of a pharaoh of Egypt's Eighteenth Dynasty. The color of the leather was as deep and rich as if it had just been dyed.

Wilbour sent a telegram to Gaston Maspero. He had found the tomb robber.

The police arrested Ahmed and Hussein Abd el-Rassul and kept them in prison for months. Ahmed was interrogated and tortured but he did not break. He stuck to the story that he had gone down the shaft in the cliff wall that day in 1871 to rescue a lost goat.

A hearing was held and the villagers of Qurnah turned out for the Abd el-Rassul family. One by one, the villagers paraded through court, proclaiming how innocent and upstanding Ahmed was. He was set free.

Director Maspero was furious. He was convinced the Abd el-Rassul family knew the location of a major archaeological find, but now they were free to continue to pillage it. However, there was little Director Maspero could do about the situation. He had business in Paris, so he left his assistant, Emile Brugsch, in charge.

Shortly after Director Maspero left the country, Brugsch got word that one of the Abd el-Rassul brothers was ready to talk. It was neither Ahmed nor Hussein. Mohammed, the oldest brother, had decided to turn informant.

———◆———

Why did Mohammed betray his brother?

A family argument. As compensation for enduring torture and jail time, Ahmed demanded half of the tomb's treasure.

Also, authorities offered a reward for information leading to the location of the tomb. Mohammed was convinced that it was only a matter of time before someone in the family spilled the beans. He decided to act first and claim the reward.

When Brugsch heard Mohammed's story, he decided to place the tomb under government control to prevent any more theft.

On July 5, 1881, he followed Mohammed and a gang of Arab workers to Deir el-Bahri. Brugsch was armed. The economy of Qurnah depended on grave robbery. The villagers would not take kindly to the government taking over a priceless discovery in their backyard.

The men climbed the steep cliff path. Then, Mohammed pointed at a hole covered with stones. It was so well hidden that Brugsch understood why the tomb had been undetected for 3,000 years. Mohammed removed a coil of rope from his shoulder and let it slither into the hole. Brugsch grabbed it and slid down, hand over hand.

When Brugsch's feet finally hit ground, he dropped the rope and lit his torch. He rounded a corner and stopped abruptly.

A huge sarcophagus sat in the center of the corridor. Brugsch thrust the torch out ahead of him. Just behind that sarcophagus was another coffin. In the dim light, Brugsch could make out the cartouche on the coffin lid—it was the sign of Sethos I.

Sethos I
photo credit: Olaf Tausch

Archaeologists had been searching for this pharaoh for decades.

As Brugsch continued down the corridor, the light illuminated more coffins and treasures. Porcelain, metal, and alabaster vases, cloth, and jewelry were scattered carelessly about on the floor.

Brugsch reached the massive mortuary chamber. Coffins lay this way and that. Some had been pried open. Some were stacked against the wall. Brugsch could barely breathe, but not because of the thick air from centuries past sticking in his throat.

No, Brugsch was overwhelmed with emotion as he realized that he was surrounded by some of the mightiest rulers of ancient Egypt.

Despite the heat, goosebumps rose on Brugsch's arms when he recognized the cartouche of Ramses the Great. This pharaoh had ruled Egypt for more than 60 years. According to the holy books of Judaism and Christianity, Moses, the leader of the Jewish people, had grown up in the court of Ramses the Great.

Altogether, 32 of ancient Egypt's greatest kings and queens from the Eighteenth and Nineteenth Dynasties were stored in the chamber. They were joined by court officials, princes and princesses, and royal grandchildren.

More than 6,000 funeral items were piled in the chamber. Some coffins were still covered in gold, their polished surfaces reflecting back Brugsch's own face. Later, he wrote that, "It seemed as though I was looking into the faces of my own ancestors."

But there was no time for Brugsch to daydream. This tomb was a gold mine to the poor village of the robbers. Rumors of a great treasure were already floating on the desert winds.

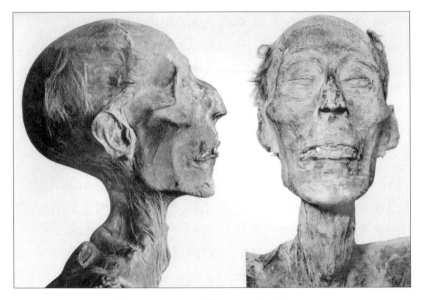

The mummy of Ramses the Great
photo credit: G. Elliot Smith

Brugsch needed to protect these mummies before thieves stole yet again.

◆

Brugsch hired a crew of 300 laborers. One by one, the mummies and funeral items were removed from the tomb. The task involved many challenges. The sarcophagus of Queen Ahmose Nefertiti was 10 feet long, and it took 16 men to shove the coffin up the shaft and haul it down the cliff.

When Ramses the Great's mummy sat in the hot sun too long, his arm contracted and rose. Workers panicked, threatening to quit the job then and there. The men eventually calmed down when they realized the ancient king was not coming back to life.

The Cache of Kings

In 48 hours, the tomb was empty. The mummies and their treasure were loaded on a steamship for the last leg of their journey. As the vessel made its way slowly up the Nile to Cairo, it created a funeral procession unique in human history.

Along the roughly 300-mile journey, Egyptians lined the riverbank to pay their respects. People walked along as if escorting their monarchs.

Once in Cairo, the mummies were stored in the Egyptian Museum, free from the threat of robbers.

Today, scientists do the work that priests used to perform as they preserve the mummies' remains. Steel and glass cases have replaced the stone and jeweled sarcophagi. The modern coffins are pumped full of gas that mimics the air of a tomb and prevents the mummies from decaying.

It took 3,000 years, but these kings and queens have reached the end of their journey. In a strange twist of fate, nineteenth-century tomb robbers exposed the work of thieves from ancient times, thereby guaranteeing the survival of the royal mummies. In a secure environment out of the reach of grave robbers, Egypt's kings and queens can finally rest in peace, closer to immortality than they have ever been.

COLOMBIA

EQUADOR

PERU

BRAZIL

● HUACA RAJADA
●LAMBAYEQUE
●CHICLAYO

PACIFIC
OCEAN

1987
Grave robbers seize
control of Huaca Rajada,
where archaeological
treasure was found,
sparking a violent
battle between
villagers and
archaeologists.

YOU
ARE
HERE

1980	1986	1987
Peru returns to civilian rule after 12 years of military government	The Bernal brothers begin looting Huaca Rajada	The Lord of Sipán is excavated by an archaeologist

Chapter Five

The Lord of Sipán

A village of poor peasants discovers an ancient tomb full of treasure. A gang of thugs seizes the site and funnels priceless artifacts to an international smuggling network. A gun-toting archeologist stands his ground, refusing to let tomb raiders sell history to the highest bidder.

This might sound like a description of the latest blockbuster movie, but it's a story straight from the history books.

In Peru, the past does not sit far from the surface. Ancient, mud-brick tombs called huacas occupy every corner of the country. One of the most famous of these, Huaca Rajada, shadows the village of Sipán on Peru's northwest coast.

A road splits this burial complex in half. On the north side of the road, two pyramids stand shoulder to shoulder 130 feet above the surrounding sugar cane fields. On the road's south side is a smaller plateau, 60 feet tall with a flat top the size of a football field.

Two thousand years ago, an army of builders from the Moche culture erected these mud-brick mounds for their nobility.

The Moche civilization controlled northern Peru from 100 to 700 CE. One of the most advanced cultures in the ancient world, the Moche made ceramics on an industrial scale and built canals that irrigated the dry land. These canals lasted into the modern age.

What drew grave robbers to Moche tombs was metalwork. These ancient people produced vast quantities of delicate copper, gold, and silver jewelry and ornaments.

The Moche were not a peaceful people. Moche art displays a culture of warriors wielding clubs and maces, sacrificing prisoners, and drinking their blood from golden goblets.

Even human sacrifices could not save the Moche from eventual destruction. Sometime around 550, catastrophe struck. Severe drought was followed by 18 months of punishing rain that flooded Moche fields and destroyed their villages.

The Lord of Sipán

Over time, other civilizations rose to power in northern Peru.

For the next 900 years, these cultures built atop Huaca Rajada. They added layer after layer of their own architecture and artifacts until the Moche had disappeared.

In the mid-twentieth century, archaeologists did a hasty excavation of Huaca Rajada. They found rough mud bricks from the Chimu civilization that had dominated Peru hundreds of years after the Moche. But rough mud bricks aren't very interesting, so the scientists and archaeologists moved on.

It was left to the tomb raiders to study the site more closely.

During the 1980s, the village of Sipán was a community of poor sugar cane farmers. The people had no running water in their houses, no paved roads, and lousy medical care. So, when the people of Sipán could not put food on their tables, they turned to Huaca Rajada for help.

Huaca del Sol, another burial complex built by the Moche civilization
photo credit: Martin St-Amant

Tomb Raiders

Looting the pyramids had been a weekend hobby for centuries. There was even a ritual to follow. A local shaman would accompany the men of the village to the huaca to dig for treasure. Before anyone plunged a shovel into the soil, the shaman made a payment of coca leaves, alcohol, tobacco, and food to the spirits of the huaca.

Then, he asked the spirits to protect the huaqueros, or tomb looters, and to lead them to treasure.

Most villagers took this ritual seriously. No one wanted angry ghosts of their long-dead ancestors causing a landslide or cave in.

When the huaqueros unearthed a fragment of cloth or a copper artifact, they sold these in Chiclayo, the largest city in the region. These small sales provided a few dollars to help carry a family over to the next sugar cane harvest.

All this changed in 1986, when the Bernal brothers seized control of Huaca Rajada. They were a new kind of grave robber.

The four Bernal brothers lived in their parents' house, a 15-minute walk from Huaca Rajada. When these men dug for treasure, they did not bother bringing a shaman along and they didn't waste time offering liquor or food.

The Lord of Sipán

The Bernal brothers weren't interested in clay pots or scraps of textiles. They were after the good stuff.

The Bernals were well known to the local police. The brothers had been in trouble for everything from automobile theft to drug trafficking to murder. They also knew antiquities dealers in Peru's largest cities, dealers with connections to criminal networks that smuggled looted artifacts out of the country.

From the front yard of their parents' house, the Bernal brothers kept an eye on Huaca Rajada. If any villager happened to unearth something big, the Bernals would be ready.

That day came in November 1986, when 36-year-old Ernil Bernal heard that a huaquero had made a special discovery.

Ricardo Zapata's elderly mother lived in a thatched hut at the foot of the shortest pyramid at Huaca Rajada. Zapata dug there regularly and had uncovered lots of copper ornaments. Ernil Bernal ordered Zapata to stay off the huaca. When Zapata objected, Ernil put a pistol to Zapata's temple and said if he did not buzz off, Ernil would kill him and his mother. Ricardo obeyed.

The Bernal brothers and their gang of huaqueros went digging every night and refused to allow any other huaqueros on site. They uncovered animal bones, a few ceramic pots, and tiny gold beads.

The beads excited everyone, but as November turned into December and then January, the huaqueros became discouraged. The tunnels were cramped and full of mosquitos. Men became sick and lost faith. Some got spooked. Had they angered the spirits of the huaca?

Ernil Bernal refused to quit digging. His energy and motivation came from more than a hunger for treasure. Ernil was a drug addict, a longtime user of hallucinogenic mushrooms and the mind-altering sap of the San Pedro plant.

"He was a strange guy," said a friend. "He would talk to you all the time about flying saucers. . . . He took San Pedro every night." Ernil also dug for loot on the huaca every night.

At 10:30 p.m. on February 6, 1987, he found what he was looking for.

Ernil couldn't see the moon or the stars, only dirt. He was crawling in the toe of a boot-shaped pit 23 feet inside the shortest pyramid of Huaca Rajada. Ernil reached one hand up and ran his fingers over the adobe bricks that lined the tunnel ceiling. He felt it—a peanut-shaped lump in the mortar between two bricks. Using his fingernails, Ernil plucked out a golden bead.

The Lord of Sipán

Moche pyramid builders had tossed these beads into wet mortar to please their gods.

The beads pleased the huaqueros, too—they called them "seeds from heaven." In seconds, Ernil had a handful of gold beads. Dropping them into a bag around his waist, he raised the lantern to inspect the ceiling.

The color of the bricks looked different in this spot, as if the builders had switched from one type of clay to another. Setting down the lantern, Ernil wiped his sweaty forehead and grabbed a 4-foot, T-shaped rod. He gripped it tightly and drove the rod up into the ceiling with all his might.

He had expected to strike hard clay bricks, but instead, the T-rod slid in smoothly up to its hilt. Ernil lost his balance and fell on his knees. Dry white sand streamed down through the hole in the ceiling, causing swirls of dust to spin around him. In seconds, the sand stream became an avalanche, burying Ernil in soil and bricks.

Cave-ins like this were the reason most huaqueros brought a shaman and offerings to a dig.

Luckily for Ernil, a couple of other men in the gang were digging nearby. When they heard the tunnel collapse, they called out to Ernil. He managed to croak out a sandy response. Seconds later, Ernil heard the sounds of their frantic digging and shafts of light from their lanterns illuminated the now roofless tunnel he was lying in.

Ernil blinked several times to clear the grit from his eyes. The huaqueros stood around the edge of the pit, staring down at him. At first, Ernil thought they were afraid any more digging might cause another avalanche. But it was not fear on the men's faces. It was awe. Ernil was buried up to his shoulders in treasure.

"After that night," Samuel Bernal said, "no one said Ernil was crazy anymore."

It turns out, Ernil had dug into a tomb from underneath, causing the floor of the burial chamber to collapse on his head. He had uncovered treasure beyond his wildest imaginings.

Tiny statues of men adorned in turquoise. Cat masks of hammered gold. A golden jaguar head attached to a string of gold beads shaped like tiny owls. Scores of gold and silver peanuts. A huge, gold back flap, the armor worn by Moche royalty during ceremonies.

"It was like a hallucination," said Samuel Bernal.

Every artifact was passed from man to man and placed into a nylon sack. When the sack was filled, one of the looters carried it to his car. The bag went in the trunk and the looter immediately drove to the Bernals' house. There, they stashed their find in a wooden cupboard in the hallway. The gold back flap was too large for the cupboard, so it went under the dirt in the chicken coop.

By morning, the huaqueros had hauled out 11 sacks of treasure. After locking the cupboard and giving the key to their mother for safekeeping, the Bernal brothers went to bed.

Luck had led the Bernal brothers to the treasure of Sipán, but greed took it from them.

Word spread quickly that the huaqueros had hit the jackpot. The next morning, Huaca Rajada was swarming with locals and people from nearby villagers. The Bernal brothers chased people off the huaca at gunpoint, but knew they needed to give the villagers something so no one would squeal to the cops.

The gang passed out some of the little gold beads they had discovered and allowed villagers to enter pits the Bernals had already excavated and dig for 15 minutes. If a villager did not reemerge at the 15-minute mark, Ernil threatened to bury them alive.

Samuel Bernal was in charge of selling the artifacts. The Bernals had worked with a dealer before—a former police officer known simply as Pereda. Bernal contacted Pereda and the man put out the word that he had something special to sell. Only days after the brothers' discovery, international collectors were knocking on Pereda's door.

According to Peruvian law, it was illegal to steal ancient artifacts and to purchase them. But the law had a major loophole. As soon as a collector "registered" his artifacts with the government's National Institute of Culture, he became their legal owner. This law punished the poor peasants who dug artifacts out of the ground while protecting wealthy antiquities collectors.

However, collectors were not allowed to export artifacts. A dealer such as Pereda could buy looted art and quickly register it to make it legal, but the second he tried to ship the item to a rich collector outside the country, the authorities would confiscate it.

With more than 5,000 known archaeological sites in Peru, the country was too poor to excavate and protect all of them. The best the government could hope for was to keep Peru's past in Peru.

However, crooked dealers got around this obstacle by smuggling. Within a few weeks, the Sipán treasure was making its way into the homes and galleries of collectors around the world.

Smuggling was not the Bernal brothers' game. They were only interested in off-loading their loot to Pereda and getting cash for it.

The Lord of Sipán

A few days after they had emptied the burial chamber, Ernil and a few of his gang members laid the loot out in the sugar cane field behind the Bernals' house. Ernil insisted that he and his brothers should get nine of the 11 sacks of treasure. The other men disagreed and accused Ernil of holding back some of the good stuff.

There are several stories of what happened, but one thing is certain. Shots were fired, and one of the huaqueros was killed. Another looter ran from Ernil and hid in the sugar cane field. When the coast was clear, that man ran straight to the police and spilled the beans.

This looter helped save a piece of Peruvian history.

The loud knocks on the door woke Dr. Walter Alva from a fitful sleep the night of February 25, 1987.

The 35-year-old director of the Brüning Museum lived in the town of Lambayeque. The cottage where he lived with his wife and two sons was located behind the museum.

Alva had a bad case of bronchitis and only wanted to roll over and go back to sleep, but the pounding on the door grew more insistent. Alva threw back the bedcovers and heaved himself out of bed.

When Alva opened his door, Benedicto, the night watchman of the museum, stood on the front step.

The chief of police for the Department of Lambayeque, where Sipán was located, had called the museum. He wanted Alva to report immediately to headquarters in Chiclayo, the region's capital city. It was a 35-minute drive away.

Alva called the police department. "I am very sick and cannot go anywhere."

"What we have here," said the deputy chief of police, "is sure to make your fever go away."

In addition to directing the Brüning Museum, Walter Alva was also the inspector general of archaeology for Lambayeque. His job was to track the movement and sale of stolen artifacts.

Alva had a reputation for fighting tirelessly to protect archaeological sites. He lectured schoolchildren and spoke to the media and tried to stir up Peruvian's pride in their past. Alva believed huaqueros had been raised to scorn their own history, and he wanted to stop grave robbing to preserve Peru's cultural identity.

As he hung up the phone, Alva was skeptical. What could be so important to drag him from his sick bed in the middle of the night? But he dressed and climbed into the museum's van.

The Lord of Sipán

As Benedicto drove onto the highway, Alva leaned his head against the window. Beyond his reflection in the glass, the rice and sugar cane fields were only a dark blur. The landscape was completely flat, except where huacas hulked like giants in the night.

When Alva arrived at headquarters, the chief of police filled him in on recent events. A huaquero had tipped off the cops that the Bernals had looted Huaca Rajada. When the police searched the Bernals' property, they found a sack full of artifacts hidden in a hallway cupboard.

The chief handed Alva a brown paper package. The archaeologist hefted its weight and guessed it weighed about three pounds. A ceramic pot? Alva sighed. He had seen thousands of pots through the years. He hadn't needed to get out of his bed for this.

But when Alva unwrapped the package, he almost dropped it in shock. Inside was an intricately carved human head made of hammered gold. The silver eyes had pupils of rare lapis lazuli, a deep-blue stone.

This was no ordinary artifact. This piece of royal Moche art was worth a king's ransom.

And there was more. Another package held the golden head of a puma with teeth of polished seashells and teardrop eyes of gold. There were gold and silver nose rings shaped like crescent moons, huge gold and silver peanuts sculpted like the real nuts, and an 8-inch gold rattle with the figure of a Moche god carved on it.

Alva was speechless. The huaqueros had discovered the tomb of a Moche lord.

The next day, Alva, and his assistant, Luis Chero, joined the police when they returned to search the Bernal house again. None of the brothers were home, but their father permitted the search. The police looked through the entire house and yard, but they walked right past the chicken coop. No artifacts were found.

From the Bernals' house, Alva and Chero went on to Huaca Rajada and were horrified at what they found there. Hundreds of villages were climbing over the pyramids, heaving pickaxes and shovels as they dug for more treasure. The hill was so pockmarked it resembled the surface of the moon. When the police drove up, the villagers barely raised their heads.

The deputy police chief sped down the road that cut through the pyramid complex, his siren blaring. His car screeched to a halt, swirls of dust rising from the tires. None of the huaqueros quit digging.

The deputy chief ordered his men to shoot bursts of machine gun fire into the air. Looters on the largest pyramid fired their own volley in return, and the police had to dive for cover.

Finally, the deputy chief ordered his officers down into the tunnels to arrest the huaqueros. Looters scrambled down the pyramids and disappeared into the sugar cane fields while others crawled from tunnel to tunnel. After 30 minutes of chaos, the looters cleared off and peace finally descended.

Now, it was finally Alva and Chero's turn. The archaeologists searched through at least 30 pits before they finally found the one the Bernals had excavated. As soon as he climbed down into it, Alva knew the space had been a burial chamber. He recognized the sour, acrid odor of a tomb. But all that remained of the final resting place of a Moche lord were bone dust and bits pf pottery.

The police and Luis Chero assumed Alva would order the pits on Huaca Rajada filled in. After all, it seemed clear the huaqueros had stolen every artifact. Their assumptions were wrong.

Archaeologists had made a serious mistake some years earlier when they concluded that Huaca Rajada had little archeological value. Alva would not make that mistake again.

On March 2, about a week after authorities chased huaqueros off the site, Alva pitched a tent at the entrance to the tunnel Ernil Bernal had dug. He was moving in. Alva believed that even if all the treasure had been looted, Huaca Rajada had much more to teach him.

To protect the site from further looting, two uniformed policemen patrolled the huaca 24 hours a day. To protect himself, Alva carried a gun.

The huaqueros were still at large. The police had raided the Bernal house three more times, but turned up only fragments of artifacts. Meanwhile, Ernil Bernal hung out at taverns in Sipán, passing out gold beads to guys at the bar and spinning outrageous tales of the riches still buried in Huaca Rajada.

Villagers saw Ernil as a modern-day Robin Hood. Ernil told a reporter, "I am the voice of the poor. The treasures of Huaca Rajada are the treasures of our ancestors. They belong to us."

That was a load of nonsense to Walter Alva. He said most of the peasants had no appreciation of Moche culture or Peruvian history. They just wanted gold. But the villagers resented Alva's takeover of the huaca. By day, they stood outside the barbed wire surrounding the site, shouting swearwords and throwing bottles.

By night, they tried to sneak onto the huaca.

Meanwhile, Ernil Bernal was rapidly deteriorating. The drugs and booze he was hooked on worsened a mental illness he had been struggling with for years.

Ernil often went into trances. Sometimes, he trembled violently and screamed that he was being chased by men or attacked by swarms of insects. Ernil was terrified the spirits of Huaca Rajada were coming to take their revenge on him for defiling their tomb.

Goods were slowly entering the antique market that Alva realized were royal Moche artifacts that could only have come from Sipán. This was evidence that the Bernals had stolen more treasure than Alva or the police realized.

Another raid on the Bernal house was scheduled. The treasure must be there somewhere.

At 5 a.m. on April 11, Alva and a television crew rode in the museum van in the rear of a police motorcade. As the vehicles arrived at the Bernal house, the police cars cut their lights and waited. The television crew had asked the officers to hold off their raid until the sun came up.

They needed better lighting.

Before the sky got light, Carlos Bernal Vargas, the father of the Bernal family, emerged from the house to milk his cows. When Vargas spotted the police cars, he shouted a warning. His cries alerted the Bernals' dog, which began to bark. The barking woke Ernil's mother.

Seconds later, the police spotted two figures darting along the side of the house and heading for the sugar cane fields.

The police gave chase and shots were fired. The family dog was hit, the older brother, Juan, was grazed by a bullet, and Ernil was shot in the back. He staggered a few paces and collapsed under an avocado tree. Officers surrounded Ernil. "Where did you bury the loot?" they shouted.

Ernil lost consciousness without saying a word. A few hours later, he died in the hospital. The bullets had pierced his liver.

The villagers of Sipán called the incident Ernil's "murder," and it was front-page news across Peru. Walter Alva was made the villain of the story. When Ernil's funeral procession passed Huaca Rajada, people shouted curses at Alva and demanded the "thieves" and "murderers" be removed from the huaca.

Alva was deeply disturbed by Ernil's death. He understood the economic reasons that pushed poor peasants to loot tombs. He realized his relationship with the villagers had been permanently poisoned. But Alva refused to apologize for trying to stop the huaqueros from robbing graves. He said the Bernal brothers and their gang had "in one night . . . destroyed a tomb that would have taken us a year to excavate."

With the local villagers angry because of Ernil's death, everyone assumed Alva would seal the huaca and move on to another archaeological site. Instead, he called a meeting of his museum sponsors.

"I'm not leaving Huaca Rajada," he announced. "I'm going to excavate."

The excavation of Huaca Rajada began during the middle of April 1987. Alva shocked everyone by hiring a well-known huaquero named Marcial Montessa as the site foreman.

Alva trusted the 23-year-old man. Before the excavation began, Alva had gone door to door throughout Sipán, telling villagers to apply for jobs at the site. They slammed their doors in his face. But on the morning of April 16, Montessa showed up in front of Alva's tent and asked for a job. Alva hired him.

Soon, more locals showed up to apply for work. Relations between Alva and the locals were still bad, but this was a change for the better.

The excavation struggled to survive. It had a bare-bones budget. When Alva ran out of funds, he paid his staff in beer and noodles.

An international antiquities dealer with connections to organized crime warned Susana Alva that if she did not convince her husband to leave Huaca Rajada, he would be murdered. But Susana was an archaeologist, too, and she refused to be pushed around.

"If you kill Walter, then I'll take his place," she shouted at the man. "And if you kill me, then there'll be someone else to take my place."

photo credit: Gusjer

The Lord of Sipán

Despite everyone's grit and determination, something had to change or the excavation of Huaca Rajada would have to close down, and then the looters would move in.

That change came on June 14. Excavators began to uncover hundreds of clay pots, beakers, jars, and vases, all of Moche design. Then, in a small niche in the bottom of the chamber, they discovered the skeleton of a man.

In a nearby chamber, pieces of a copper headdress were unearthed. Alva and Cherno thought the man was either a victim of sacrifice or someone who committed suicide to be buried with his king.

So where was the king?

Artifacts that are thousands of years old are very fragile, so the excavation moved at a snail's pace. But by the end of June, Alva had uncovered traces of wooden beams and copper straps in the shape of a 7-by-4-foot rectangle—an unopened coffin.

Word of the find flew through the village. On July 1, 1987, swarms of protestors stood behind the barbed wire fence demanding their "ancestors' inheritance."

Some members of Alva's crew of workers tried to convince Alva that the only safe thing to do was dig around the coffin and take the entire block of earth to the museum to be excavated. The villagers were so angry, who knew what would happen? Alva refused. He wanted the people to witness their ancestor's rebirth.

With tweezers, trowels, and teaspoons, Alva and Chero removed dirt and sediment. Slowly, the "Lord of Sipán" emerged. Decayed textiles with panels of gilded copper. Gold ingots. Copper spear points. A sheet of gilded copper shaped like a man's torso.

Thousands of white, pink, and green shell beads. Ear ornaments of gold with turquoise inlay. Peanut-shaped beads of gold.

Finally, when the last layer of dirt had been brushed away, a skeleton appeared.

The man had practically been embalmed in gold. Thin gold sheets covered his face and filled the inside of his mouth. A golden headrest cradled his skull. A necklace of gold disks hugged his neck and his feet wore sandals of solid silver.

This was the Lord of Sipán.

More analysis of the tomb would have to wait. The morning of July 11, 1987, angry villagers tried to storm the site. Police lobbed teargas canisters at them and the crowd hid in the sugar cane fields, arming themselves with picks, shovels, and tire irons.

Alva decided the best way to prove to the villagers that he was trying to preserve something priceless was to invite the locals to see the burial for themselves.

The next morning, Alva walked down the huaca and up to the barbed wire fence. He stood face to face with Alberto Jaime, one of the loudest protestors. Alva told Jaime that his inheritance was waiting at the top of the pyramid. He should hurry and "help himself" before anyone else "stole it."

The crowd was stunned. This was not what they had expected.

Then, Alva removed a wire cutter from his pocket and snipped the barrier separating him and Jaime. He reached through the opening, grabbed the man by the collar, and pulled him toward the platform where the Lord of Sipán lay. The villagers followed.

At the top of the platform, everyone stood around the opening to the burial chamber. Jaime peered down at the exposed artifacts. Alva pushed a shovel into his hands and dared him to "steal from his ancestors."

Tomb Raiders

Then Alva began to lecture. He told the villagers that long ago, "A great lord of the Moche civilization" had made this spot his headquarters.

"His people dressed him in gold," Alva shouted. He reached down and plucked a large gold bead from the burial chamber and handed it to Jaime. "Nothing less was good enough for the exalted Lord of Sipán."

A sort of magic happened that day because of Alva's powerful words. Many of the villagers finally understood. No longer was Huaca Rajada just a hill full of treasure, there for the taking.

Huaca Rajada was the burial place of the Lord of Sipán. A human being. A man. One of their ancestors.

In 2002, the Royal Tombs of Sipán Museum in Lambayeque, Peru, opened its doors. The museum is shaped like a huaca. Visitors enter a ramp that leads to the top of the building and work their way down terraces and slopes to the burial chamber of the Lord of Sipán. There, the king rests in the remains of his sarcophagus. He is still regal thousands of years after death. Walter Alva hoped the museum would help the Peruvian people "feel that they are really the heirs to a great culture." A culture the public would cherish rather than loot.

Glossary

accomplice: a person who helps someone commit a crime.

ambitious: having a strong desire to succeed.

amulet: a small piece of jewelry worn as protection against evil.

anatomy: the structure of the human body.

ancient: from a long time ago, more than 1,500 years ago.

antiquities: objects of art from the ancient past.

apprehend: to arrest someone for a crime.

apprentice: a period of training during which a young person learns a trade from an experienced worker.

archaeologist: a person who studies ancient people through the objects they left behind.

architect: a person who designs buildings.

arrogant: having an exaggerated sense of one's own importance or abilities.

artifact: an object made by a human being in an earlier time.

assassination: to kill someone.

bacteria: tiny microbes that live in animals, plants, soil, and water. Bacteria are decomposers that help decay food. Some bacteria are harmful and others are helpful.

bazaar: a market in a Middle Eastern country.

BCE: put after a date, BCE stands for Before Common Era and counts years down to zero.

black market: the illegal buying and selling of products.

bloodletting: a form of medical treatment that involved cutting a vein or applying leeches to the skin in order to draw out sickness.

bribe: a gift, often money, to get someone to do something wrong and often illegal.

bust: a sculpture of a person's head, shoulders, and chest.

cache: a collection of similar items that are stored or hidden away.

cadaver: a dead body.

canal: a man-made waterway.

cannibalism: eating a human being.

carbon: a nonmetal element found in all organic material.

carcass: a dead body.

cargo: goods or materials that are carried or transported by a vehicle.

casket: a coffin.

castaway: a person who has been shipwrecked and stranded in an isolated place.

catacomb: an underground cemetery consisting of tunnels and chambers to house coffins.

CE: put after a date, CE stands for Common Era and counts up from zero. This book was printed in 2018 CE.

ceramics: items made from clay.

cesspool: a container to store waste.

chant: to repeat a sound over and over.

Glossary

chaos: a state of complete confusion.

charter: a document that protects the king's subjects from unfair actions.

civilization: a community of people that is advanced in art, science, and government.

climate: the average weather patterns in an area during a long period of time.

coax: to convince someone to do something.

colonist: a settler living in a new land.

colony: an area that is controlled by or belongs to another country.

coney men: men involved in criminal counterfeit money operations.

confederacy: an alliance.

Confederate: a supporter of the Confederate States of America, the union of 11 states that broke from the nation in 1861 and fought for independence from the United States.

confiscate: when someone in authority seizes property.

conspiracy: a plot.

contaminate: to pollute or make dirty.

corpse: a dead body.

corrupt: the dishonest or illegal behavior of people in power.

counterfeit: replicas of money intended to fool people into thinking the money is real.

crop: a plant grown for food or other uses.

crypt: an underground chamber used to hold a dead body.

culture: the beliefs and customs of a group of people.

currency: the system of money used in a country.

decay: to break down and rot.

deceased: dead.

denomination: the value of a coin or bill.

devour: to eat hungrily or greedily.

discipline: control gained through training and hard work.

disembark: to get off a ship or airplane.

dissect: to cut something apart to study what is inside.

drought: a long period of time without rain.

dynasty: a series of rulers from the same family.

dysentery: a painful, sometimes fatal, disorder of the intestines characterized by severe diarrhea.

edible: able to be eaten without harm.

emaciated: abnormally thin or weak.

embalm: to treat a dead body with chemicals to prevent it from rotting.

engraver: in counterfeit operations, the engraver was an artist who carved an exact replica of a dollar bill on a metal plate from which paper copies could be printed.

entrails: a person's internal organs.

Glossary

erode: to wear away.

etch: to mark a hard material.

eternity: forever.

excavate: to carefully remove soil from an area in order to discover what is underneath.

excrement: human or animal waste.

exhume: to dig up a corpse from the ground.

expedition: a journey undertaken by a group of people with a specific purpose.

exports: goods sent to be sold in other countries.

famine: a period of great hunger and lack of food for a large population.

fate: the development of events beyond a person's control.

flagship: the ship in a fleet that carries the commander.

fledgling: just getting started.

fleet: a group of ships traveling together.

forensic: relating to the investigation of a crime.

forgery: a fake.

fungi: mold, mildew, rust, and mushrooms. Plural of fungus.

gold rush: when people rush somewhere gold has been found.

gruesome: something horrible and bloody.

hallucinogenic: a drug that causes a person to see something that is not real.

havoc: widespread destruction.

hieroglyphics: the picture writing of ancient Egyptians.

hostile: very unfriendly, relating to an enemy.

huaca: an ancient tomb.

huaqueros: tomb robbers.

hull: the body of a ship.

hurricane: a bad storm with high winds.

hymn: a religious song of praise and worship.

immortality: to live forever.

industrial scale: to produce massive quantities of a product.

informant: a person who gives information to another.

intrigue: to arouse the curiosity or interest of someone.

investor: a person or organization that puts money into a business or property, with the expectation of future profit.

irrigate: to supply land with water, usually for crops.

isthmus: a narrow strip of land bordered by water on both sides, joining two larger land areas.

labyrinth: a maze of corridors and passageways.

larceny: theft.

latrine: a bathroom that can be used by several people at once, often as simple as a long trench dug in the earth.

livestock: animals raised for food and other uses.

longboat: a large boat powered by oars.

malaria: a disease spread by infected mosquitoes. It is found mainly in the hot areas near the equator.

Glossary

malnutrition: poor nutrition caused by not eating the right foods.

mangle: to damage by cutting, tearing, or crushing.

mason: a bricklayer.

memorabilia: items kept to remember someone by.

militia: a military force staffed by civilians instead of a regular army.

millennium: a period of 1,000 years.

molar: a flattened, square-shaped tooth at the back of the jaw, used for chewing or grinding.

morsel: a small bit of food.

mourn: to grieve.

mummy: a dead body that has been preserved so that it doesn't decay.

necropolis: a huge cemetery.

negotiate: to reach an agreement, compromise, or treaty through bargaining and discussing.

nobility: the upper class of many societies.

Northern Hemisphere: the half of the earth north of the equator.

obelisk: a stone pillar with a pyramid top.

odious: repulsive.

offensive: an attacking military campaign.

organic: something that is or was living.

palisade: a fence made of rows of pointed posts.

papyrus: a form of paper made in ancient Egypt.

parasite: a plant or animal that feeds on another plant or animal without directly killing it.

peasant: a farmer in feudal society who lived on and farmed land owned by his lord.

peninsula: a piece of land that juts out into water.

petition: to formally request something.

pharaoh: an ancient Egyptian king.

pillage: to steal.

pitch: a substance that is made from tar.

plateau: a large, raised area that is fairly flat.

platoon: a unit of soldiers.

plot: an illegal plan.

plunder: to steal.

polls: the location where people vote.

preserve: to store something in a way that protects it from rotting.

prey: an animal hunted by another animal.

profit: the money made by selling an item or service for more than it cost.

provision: food, drink, or equipment for a long journey.

prow: the part of a ship's bow that is out of the water.

pyramid: a large stone structure with a square base and triangular sides.

ransom: money demanded for the return of a captured person.

ravenous: starving.

Glossary

ravine: a deep river valley carved by running water.

rector: a church official.

register: to enter onto an official list.

remote: far-away and isolated.

riot: an out-of-control gathering of people protesting something.

roper: a former criminal who worked for the police as a paid informant.

sacrifice: the killing of a person or animal as an offering to a god.

salvation: being saved from sin, evil, harm, or destruction.

sarcophagus: a large, stone box containing an Egyptian king's coffin and mummy.

sediment: loose rock particles such as sand or clay.

shaft: a tunnel or passage.

shaman: a person believed to have the ability to communicate with the spirit world and the living world.

shover: a counterfeit operator who purchases goods with fake money.

shroud: a cover for something that conceals it from view.

slaughterhouse: a place to butcher animals.

slave: a person owned by another person and forced to work without pay, against their will.

smuggle: to transport goods illegally into and out of a country.

social rank: describes the level of wealth of a person in a society.

specimen: a sample used for study.

spirit: the soul.

supplement: to add to.

surgeon: a doctor who performs operations.

suspense: a feeling or state of nervousness or excitement caused by wondering what will happen.

tannery: a place where animal skins are processed.

temple: the flat part of either side of the head between the forehead and the ear.

tide: the daily rise and fall of the ocean's water level near a shore.

till: to plow.

tomb: a room or place where a dead person is buried.

toxic: poisonous.

trade: the exchange of goods for other goods or money.

traitor: someone who is disloyal and abandons or betrays a group or cause.

typhoid: a highly contagious and often deadly disease caused by bacteria. Symptoms include fever, diarrhea, and headaches.

vainglorious: too much pride in oneself.

vault: a large sealed container that houses a casket.

vengeance: getting even.

vermin: small animals or insects that are pests, such as cockroaches or mice.

victual: food.

Resources

Books

Putnam, James. *Mummy*. DK Witness, 2009.

Sheinkin, Steve. *Lincoln's Grave Robbers*. Scholastic Press, 2012.

Walker, Sally M. *Written in Bone: Buried Lives of Jamestown and Colonial Maryland*. Carolrhoda Books, 2009.

Websites

Explore the clues behind the plot to kill President Lincoln. *Killing Lincoln*. National Geographic Channel. *killinglincoln.nationalgeographic.com*

Take a digital tour of historic Jamestown. *historicjamestowne.org/visit/plan-your-visit/fort-site*

Museums

The British Museum's website about ancient Egypt *ancientegypt.co.uk/menu.html*

Videos

Learn more about Abraham Lincoln's death with this video. *smithsonianchannel.com/videos/the-plot-to-kidnap-lincoln/35264*

Read an article about extracting DNA from ancient Egyptian mummies. *smithsonianmag.com/science-nature/ ancient-mummies-finally-give-their-genetic-secrets-180963518*

What did the Lord of Sipán actually look like? Check it out in this newscast. *pocho.com/this-is-the-face-of-perus-lord-of-sipan-2000-year -old-warrior-priest-video*

Explore more about the history of body snatching in this video. "Cemetery Alarm." History Detectives, PBS. Season 7, Episode 3. *pbs.org/opb/historydetectives/video/1169415042*